SCOTTISH BICYCLES & TRICYCLES

Alastair Dodds

NMS Publishing

Published by NMS Publishing Limited, Royal Museum, Chambers Street, Edinburgh EH1 1JF
© NMS Publishing Limited 1999
Series editor Iseabail Macleod

Other titles available in this series	*Fishing & Whaling*	*Sporting Scotland*
	Farming	*Spinning & Weaving*
	Building Railways	*Making Cars*
	Leaving Scotland	*Feeding Scotland*
	Going to School	*Going to Church*
	Scots in Sickness & Health	*Going on Holiday*
	Going to Bed	*Shipbuilding*
	Scotland's Inland Waterways	
Forthcoming titles	*Getting Married in Scotland*	*Scottish Music Hall, Variety and*
	Scottish Cinema	*Pantomime*
	Scottish Engineering	*Iron & Steel*
Other titles by the author include	*Making Cars*	

British Library Cataloguing in Publication Data
A catalogue record of this book is available from the British Library
ISBN 1 901663 21 3
Designed by NMS Publishing Limited
Printed in Great Britain by Cambridge University Press Printing Division

Acknowledgements
The author is grateful to all those who have helped in making this book possible, including: Barry Branden, Alex Brown, Alex Cross, Sandy Lindsay, Sarah Phillips, Jack Potter, Charles Ralph, John Robertson, John Smith, Lottie Smith, Isobel Stewart, Meredith Williamson, Douglas and Ina Wilson, Ernie Worrall. Also to the staff at Edinburgh Bicycle Co-op, Glasgow Museums, Glenalmond College, Hawick Museum, Shetland Museum, George Watsons College and members of the Scottish Section of the Veteran-Cycle Club. Finally thanks to my ever-helpful wife Anne for her constant encouragement and useful comments.

Illustrations: 7, 9, 29, 31, 32, 33, 38, 40, 49, 50, 51, 54, 62, 67, 68: National Museums of Scotland. 12, 44, 63, 65, 71, 73: Alex Brown. 14, 25, 26: Glasgow Museums & Art Galleries. 16: Dumfries Museum. 19: Peter Matthews, Dublin. 23, 47: Glenalmond College, Perthshire. 30: Charles Waterston. 36: Alastair Cunningham. 43 Nicholas Oddy. 57, 58, 59, 77, 79, 80, 81: Lottie & John Smith. 64, 72: Douglas & Ina Wilson. 75: John Robertson. 83, 84, 86: Edinburgh Bicycle Cooperative, Bruntsfield, Edinburgh. 88: Sarah Phillips.

Illustrations captioned SLA are from the Scottish Life Archive in the National Museums of Scotland.

Cover picture: *Detail from a Howe Machine Co poster, c1885*

Contents

Introduction

Scotland has never been an easy country to travel around. At the beginning of the nineteenth century very few people owned their own transport and even hired transport was beyond the reach of most people. Until the coming of the railways most people walked. Sometimes a longer journey might be undertaken by boat, or a farmer might own a horse or ox to draw a market cart. But unless they were very wealthy most people simply had no choice but to walk. The privileged few still had to rely on a beast to ride or to draw a vehicle, and this posed the problem of having to provide it with food and shelter. Even the best horse had a limited range, particularly when hauling a coach.

However, even prior to 1800 people were experimenting with other means of transport, including human power and steam vehicles. Scottish-born William Murdoch built a model three-wheeled steam carriage in 1784 while working in Cornwall. Two years later another Scot, William Symington, demonstrated a steam carriage model in Edinburgh, basing its design on the horse-drawn carriages of the period. There is a story that William Murdoch had also been involved with some form of velocipede built by his father John. In contrast to William's steam model, which survives today, little is known about his father's vehicle. Local tales suggest that the machine used 'propelling poles' and that young William used to ride on it the two miles from the family home at Bello Mill, near Lugar in Ayrshire, to Cumnock.

Most of the local histories describe the machine as a 'wooden horse on wheels' and that it was built 'sometime before 1711', which was long before William was born in 1754. A poem written about William in 1817 cryptically refers to the machine in the line 'Who rode a horse no mortal e'er could tire'. There is no particular reason to doubt that some form of human-powered machine was built by the Murdoch family but what form it took, and the number of wheels that it had, will probably never be known.

Experiments in human power had been seen periodically throughout Europe from as early as 1520. These were invariably existing carriages that were modified to be driven by treadles, handles or levers powered by some unfortunate coachmen. Even the finest carriages prior to the middle of the nineteenth century were heavy and clearly there was going to be no future in this line of development. The horseless carriage would have to wait for the development of the lightweight steam engine and ultimately the petrol engine.

Human-powered vehicles were mostly seen as party tricks for the rich. Obviously only the very rich could afford to experiment with modified carriages and, for the most part, as gentlemen they would not wish to be seen strenuously exerting themselves in public. The one type of vehicle which might have been within the means of an enterprising mechanic would have been a two-wheeler. However, the only known vehicles using two wheels were carts and because the wheels were mounted at each end of an axle a horse was needed to support the front. All this was set to change with the simple realisation that one wheel could be mounted in front of the other.

Today there are an estimated 800 million bicycles in the world, twice the number of cars. But then, as we shall see, the bicycle has been around for a lot longer than the motor car.

The Dandy years

Despite the many firsts that can be claimed by the Scots the discovery of the in-line two-wheel vehicle, which would lead eventually to the bicycle of today, was not a Scottish one. It was to be a German, Baron Karl von Drais of Karlsruhe, who made this important step forward. Around 1813 von Drais, like many before him, was experimenting with human-powered carriages. His first 'Fahrmaschine' or 'driving machine' required two servants to power what was a very heavy and complicated vehicle. However, unlike most of the other inventors, he realised that what was needed was a much lighter type of vehicle.

What gave him his idea was probably a child's toy in the form of a wooden horse with a wheel at each end, but no steering. These toys were crude developments of the old children's hobbyhorse, which had a horse's

An 1819 print showing a much-exaggerated scene of dandies out for a ride on their pedestrian hobbyhorses.

head at one end of a pole and a wheel at the other. Von Drais himself stated that the motion of riding his velocipede resembled that of a skater and this is a further indication of where his inspiration came from.

As soon as von Drais introduced steering to the device he had a practical vehicle which could be propelled by sitting astride it and running. He named it the 'Laufsmachine' or 'running machine'. The year was 1817. One of his first runs with the machine was a nine-mile trip that took under an hour; less time than the mail coach. By January 1818 he was granted a local patent and by February he had taken out a five-year French patent in Paris. Unfortunately his first real public demonstration of the machine in Paris prompted a negative report in a French paper which stated that 'the machine can never be of any real utility' and 'is only of use for children to play with'.

Later in April the first report of the Laufsmachine, or Draisienne as it was now being called, appeared in an English newspaper with more favourable comments noting that the machine 'went quicker than a man at full speed and the riders did not appear fatigued'. By now people were beginning to take an interest in the new vehicle and von Drais was managing to sell a few. The first to appear in England were seen in London by the spring of 1819. These were probably the first machines to be built by Denis Johnson, a coachmaker in Covent Garden, who had the foresight to take out an English patent in December 1818, shortly after von Drais had demonstrated his machine in Paris.

In his patent Johnson calls his machine a 'pedestrian curricle' but it soon became known as the hobbyhorse, harking back to the origins of von Drais' idea. The machine would soon also be known as the dandy-horse, a name which described many of the early proponents of this new hobby. These dandies were rich playboys and the machine was just their latest fad. Costing around £10 each these were not going to be the vehicles of the future and would largely remain as playthings.

Although it is likely that examples of Johnson's hobbyhorse would have been brought to Scotland very little is known about them. However one surviving machine, by an unknown maker, can be found in the collections of the National Museums of Scotland in Edinburgh. This was almost certainly owned by the thirteenth Earl of Eglinton who is said to have been seen as a young man using the horse at a favourite place near the stables at Eglinton Castle, the family seat in Ayrshire.

This elegant hobbyhorse is in the collections of the National Museums of Scotland and is seen in 1935 before its missing seat was replaced.

Although the Earl was only eight years old when he succeeded to the peerage on the death of his grandfather in December 1819, he was already well travelled and indeed had been born on Sicily. As a fashionable young man he would be only too well aware of the latest London fads and may have ordered his London coachbuilder to produce one of the new toys. The hobbyhorse in the NMS collections is designed with a very low top beam and could easily have been ridden by an eight year old. When Lord Lammington wrote In the Days of the Dandies in 1906 he talks about a visit he had made to the Earl's room at Eglinton Castle where he saw 'all his equipment worthy of a Dandy of the last century'. Dandies were flamboyant characters who wore bright clothes and were known for lavish entertainment. Eglinton was no exception and in 1839 he held a great medieval-style tournament at the immense cost of £30,000.

Although the maker of the Eglinton hobbyhorse is unknown, if it was indeed a London coachbuilder he would have been under the watchful eye of Denis Johnson and required to pay him a royalty. It is likely, however, that not all machines were built in London. The design was so easy to copy that many must have been home-built or produced as illegal copies by coachbuilders or cabinetmakers throughout the country. Glasgow Museums have an example, built with crude ironwork but nice wood carving, which is probably an example of Scottish local enterprise.

Another surviving machine appears to be a very close copy of a Johnson design and was formerly owned by the Duke of Argyll at Roseneath Castle. Both this and the Eglinton hobbyhorses were likely to have been built by the coachbuilders serving these titled families though it is unlikely that they would have cost any less than a Johnson machine. Many of the surviving examples were originally owned by the nobility, reflecting the high cost of purchasing a machine. Their survival is often largely due to having been kept in the closed world of a Scottish castle or English country house.

The hobbyhorse received curiously little publicity in Scotland but was undoubtedly in widespread use, judging by people's reminiscences in later years. One emigrant, writing in the Scottish American Journal in 1883, describes a group of 'Paisley chaps' who rode out of the town every Saturday. This was said to have been about 1823 and the 'chaps' were probably riding locally built copies.

Within a few years the fad for running machines began to die out and still nobody had thought about driving the wheels directly. This was probably due to a belief that it was not possible to balance and propel a two-wheeler simultaneously. However, it was a Scottish hobbyhorse that is said to have been the inspiration behind the creation of the first two-wheeler to be fitted with driving gear. This horse was owned by a Dumfries wood-turner called James Charteris and the man inspired by it was Kirkpatrick Macmillan.

The first bicycle

While the introduction of the hobbyhorse was attended with wide publicity and the filing of patents, the fitting of driving gear to the first bicycle is surrounded by myth and mystery. The popular story, as every schoolchild knows, is that a blacksmith from Dumfriesshire by the name of Kirkpatrick Macmillan invented the bicycle in 1839, or 1840, or 1841 depending on the version of the story. The story, as related in the history books, tells of this isolated country blacksmith working in his smiddy one day when a hobbyhorse is brought in for repair. Kirkpatrick then copies the machine and even builds a second example for a friend. After a period of using the machine for journeys to Dumfries he becomes exasperated with the wear and tear to his shoes and decides to add driving gear consisting of levers hung from the front of the machine which drove cranks on the rear wheel via long rods.

The problem with this standard version of events is that there is no contemporary written evidence and in the later hearsay accounts it is difficult to separate fact from fantasy. The only documentary evidence that does exist are the census returns and these place Macmillan as being resident at a brother's house in Glasgow and not at the family smiddy at Courthill, near Keir Mill, Dumfriesshire, in 1841. Even if we take the later accounts to be fact it does not help Kirkpatrick's case for there are reports of other even earlier contenders for the title of 'Inventor of the Bicycle'. The most likely of these stories relates to James Charteris from Dumfries but still actually leaves us no wiser as to who the inventor was. Various accounts credit Charteris as being the builder of a hobbyhorse, and as we have seen this is an entirely plausible tale, given that it was such an easy design to copy and that examples were in use in Scotland. In addition Charteris was a wood-turner, giving him the skills needed to build a machine.

However, a story that appears in an 1897 newspaper tells a different tale. In this article, titled 'The Origin of the Cycle', James Charteris' nephew, David Johnson, is interviewed. He relates how as a boy he had ridden as a passenger on this machine and that it was fitted with pedals or

The man who is widely credited as having built the first powered two-wheeler, Kirkpatrick Macmillan, with his children Mary and John about 1870.

stirrups driving the front wheel. Johnson goes on to say that it was not his uncle's invention, thereby eliminating the possibility that he was trying to claim this great invention for his own family. Instead he tells how Charteris had bought the bicycle in Glasgow about 1829 when he had gone there to purchase a steam boiler for his workshop. Johnson was reported as being quite positive that the bicycle was 'not propelled by setting the feet to the ground'. Could this have been the world's first bicycle, invented by an unknown Glaswegian? If the story is true then perhaps Macmillan copied it and the stories of him building a bicycle are true. However a further problem with Macmillan is that we do not know how many wheels his machine used. Johnson, on the other hand, is clear about his uncle's machine being a bicycle and not a tricycle or quadricycle, which after all would have been nothing new.

The one piece of contemporary evidence that is usually quoted as proof of Macmillan having invented a bicycle is a report, repeated in several newspapers in June 1842, of an incident which took place in Glasgow. The report appeared first in the Glasgow Argus on the 9th June as follows:

YESTERDAY, a gentleman, belonging to Dumfries-shire was placed at the Gorbals police bar, charged with riding along the pavement on a velocipede, to the obstruction of the passage, and with having, by so doing, thrown over a child. It appeared, from his statement, that he had on the day previous come all the way from Old Cumnock, a distance of 40 miles, bestriding the velocipede, and that he had performed the journey in the space of five hours. On reaching the Barony of Gorbals, he had gone upon the pavement, and was soon surrounded by a large crowd, attracted by the novelty of the machine, The child who was thrown down had not sustained any injury; and, under the circumstances, the offender was fined only 5s. The velocipede employed in this instance was very ingeniously constructed - it moved on wheels turned with the hand, by means of a crank; but, to make it ̓progress,̓ appeared to require more labour than will be compensated for by the increase of speed. This invention will not supersede the railways.

This single article tells us a lot, and yet it does not mention the name of the offender. While it might have been Macmillan visiting his brothers in Glasgow (one lived in the Gorbals) it might just as easily have been James Charteris on the bicycle he is supposed to have bought there thirteen years earlier. Whatever the article does or does not tell us it is clear that at least one person from Dumfriesshire owned a human-powered vehicle in 1842 which was capable of covering forty miles in five hours; not a bad average given the poor road conditions of the time.

Many local stories can be found, from a variety of different sources, relating to the journey to Glasgow. Many of these tales have a ring of truth to them helping to give credence to the proposition that the rider was Macmillan. The town of Cumnock in Ayrshire appears in several of the tales, as it did in stories about the Murdoch family and their 'propelling pole machine'.

The most frequently told story relates how Kirkpatrick stayed overnight here with the parish schoolmaster, John McKinnell, a student friend of one of the Macmillan brothers. He did not arrive in Cumnock until after midnight and as he rushed down McKinlay's Brae he is said to have startled James Kennedy, the local shoemaker, on his way home from courting Jean Vallance. The next morning he demonstrated the machine for the people of Cumnock by riding down Glaisnock Street at high speed with his feet over the handlebars. If this did occur he would certainly have needed to get his feet out of the way of the treadles which would have been impossible to keep up with. Many years later this would become the approved way of going down any hill on a high bicycle where there was a run-out at the bottom.

Rural Scotland may seem an unlikely place for one of the great inventions of all time to make its appearance. However there were a lot of ingenious people working in the engineering trade at that time and Scotland was perhaps the epicentre, with Glasgow being known as the 'Workshop of the Empire'. It was in Glasgow that Macmillan had served his apprenticeship working for Napiers, one of the foremost engineering and shipbuilding companies on the Clyde. Robert Napier was a great believer in education and he also encouraged his apprentices to undertake small engineering projects of their own choosing. Macmillan attended night school during his time in Glasgow where, as mentioned earlier, the census records tell us that he was in residence with a brother during 1841. Perhaps he saw and copied the velocipede in the Gorbals incident. Whether indeed Macmillan was the inventor of the bicycle or merely a copyist may never be known but it is almost certain that the inventor was Scots. The sheer number of stories suggests that there must have been quite a cottage industry building velocipedes of various types in Lowland Scotland at this time.

Possibly the worlds oldest surviving bicycle, built by Gavin Dalzell of Lesmahagow about 1846, seen at the time of its gift to Glasgow Museums in 1908.

One story concerns Robert Pow, a stonemason from Selkirk, about whom we know very little. Pow is said to have built machines between 1848 and 1850, which suggests that quite a few were made. Wooden velocipedes would have been relatively easy to build though exactly who would have bought them in the Scottish Borders at this time is debatable. Possibly they were just a series of experimental models. The other curious side of this story is why a stonemason should turn his hand to building machines requiring the skills of wood and metalworking.

One of the better-known makers, and a candidate as inventor, is Gavin Dalzell, a grocer and merchant from Lesmahagow in Lanarkshire. His first machine actually survives, albeit in a heavily rebuilt form, in the Museum of Transport in Glasgow. Whatever other claims are made about this machine it is very likely to be the oldest surviving bicycle in the world. Dalzell was born in 1811, just a year before Macmillan, and lived in Lesmahagow, just forty-three miles from Macmillan's home at Courthill near Penpont. While this might suggest the possibility of Dalzell having seen the other machine, his son always asserted that this was not the case. An article that appeared in the Scottish Cyclist magazine in 1889 claimed to have the written testimony of a letter, guaranteed by the postmark, which dated his machine as having been in existence by June 1846. Indeed the article makes a claim of further evidence in the financial accounts of a blacksmith, John Leslie, dated January 1847, for having produced the iron-work for the bicycle during the previous year. None of this evidence survives, but is probably of little consequence anyway as there are at least two claimants, Macmillan and the Charteris' Glasgow bicycle, preceding Dalzell. Even his son accepted that his father was probably not the inventor, though nor was he a copyist. We do at least know that the Dalzell machine was a two-wheeler while Macmillan's may have had three wheels.

Another Dumfriesshire man to have built bicycles in the style of Macmillan and Dalzell was Thomas McCall. Here, however, there is no claim to be the inventor but there is a connection. McCall was born in 1834 in Penpont, just two miles from the Macmillan smiddy, and claims to have been coming out of school one day about 1845 just as Kirkpatrick was passing on his machine. The young McCall then followed him as he pushed his bicycle up a long hill, giving ample time to study how the driving gear worked. After leaving school McCall became an apprentice mill-wright at Elfin Bridge, just a mile from Courthill, and during this time he bought an old hobbyhorse for five shillings and fitted cranks, rods and pedals to it. A few years later he moved to New Cumnock and built an entirely new machine, which he then used for over twenty years. It is interesting to note that all this bicycle-building activity took place in this one corner of Scotland; you will remember that the man convicted at the Gorbals Court in 1842 was said to have come from New Cumnock. John Murdoch who built a contraption 'about 1711' also came from near here.

The main difference between Thomas McCall and all the other bicycle-builders of this period is that he went into limited production. This was in 1871, by which time the French front-driving velocipede had been

Another treadle driven velocipede of the 'Scottish school', built by Thomas McCall, seen outside its usual home at Dumfries Museum.

introduced to this country, and McCall was demonstrating his machine at his new home in Kilmarnock and in Glasgow. It was during one of his visits to Glasgow that he received an order from a firm to build six along with several individual orders. It is almost certainly one of these machines sold in Glasgow which survives in the Science Museum in London today.

Even McCall had his machine copied after a photograph and letter were published in the English Mechanic and Mirror of Science journal:

> The 'Kilmarnock Velocipede' Sir - I enclose a photograph of a velocipede which meets with great approval here. I have tried it, and find it very light and easy of motion. The maker, Mr T. McCall, Langlands Street, Kilmarnock, has raced and beaten some of the ordinary two-wheeled velocipedes in Glasgow. Mechanical Hawk.

There was little that he could do about copies as neither he nor anyone else had patented the design. McCall himself built one final copy of his own design for display at the annual Stanley cycle show in 1896. It was later presented to Dumfries Museum where it can still be seen.

Sadly all this flurry of activity in south-west Scotland during the first half of the nineteenth century was to lead nowhere in design terms. This Scottish 'school' of bicycle makers had rightly decided that the correct wheel to drive was the rear one, only they had got the method wrong. Had they used a chain drive instead of treadles, rods and cranks they would have undoubtedly moved bicycle development forward, perhaps by forty years, and there might never have been an era of boneshakers or high bicycles.

The Edinburgh Tricycle

While most of the activity in south-west Scotland related to machines with two wheels it was still not clear at this time whether the bicycle or the tricycle was to be the machine of the future. In many early accounts any human-powered machine was described as a velocipede regardless of the number of wheels. This even continued into the era of the boneshaker though by then it was becoming clear that the way forward lay in the development of the two-wheeler.

Before this was finally settled there were a number of interesting tricycles built. Even Macmillan and Dalzell are said to have experimented with three wheels. No doubt there were numerous others, but it was to be an Edinburgh man, Matthew Brown, who built what was described as the 'most practical type' and put it into commercial production. He gave his machine the most unoriginal name of 'The Edinburgh Tricycle'.

Matthew Brown was involved in various trades in Edinburgh during the 1850s and 60s and listed himself in the Post Office Street Directory as a cabinetmaker, upholsterer, house agent, auctioneer, appraiser and wood merchant. Obviously an all-round entrepreneur. At least some of these businesses would have proved to be useful to someone branching out into the velocipede business. It is not known exactly when Brown built his first machine but later accounts describe it as belonging to around 1860 (another is more specific in dating it as 1865-75).

Prior to this there had been a number of makers selling four-wheeled velocipedes, the most notable being Willard Sawyer in England; some of these were of relatively light construction. Someone writing in 1874 even suggests that prior to the introduction of the bicycle the four-wheel velocipede had been widely used 'especially by artisans in going to and returning from their work'. This is a surprising statement as, like the hobby-horse before, these quadricycles were expensive and unlikely to have been affordable by the average artisan. Perhaps the fashionable machines of the 1850s were sold cheaply to the artisans of the 1860s.

But four wheels would always lose out to three given that the wooden wheels were going to be a substantial part of the overall weight. This weight was also going to be a limiting factor in the use of these machines in Scotland because of the topography. Even in the cities of Edinburgh and Glasgow the hills must have put a lot of people off the idea of using a velocipede. Even today with modern lightweight bicycles, people still have second thoughts about cycling in parts of both of these cities.

However, not everyone was discouraged by the hills and the 'Edinburgh' seems to have sold well with surviving photographs showing at least three different versions or developments. An advertisement appearing in the Scotsman newspaper in 1869 describes the tricycle as being 'pronounced by mechanics to be the Best and Lightest made, weight 50lb'. This was not a light machine by today's standards but was a reasonable enough achievement for something built predominantly of wood.

The state of the roads in Scotland at this time also limited the usefulness of the tricycle for serious journeys. But unless one was sufficiently wealthy to own and maintain a horse there was little alternative to country travel away from the rapidly developing railway system. A sixty-year-old man

The Edinburgh Tricycle circa 1865 with a man who is presumed to be Matthew Brown the designer. His left hand rests on one of the steering levers.

who had owned an 'Edinburgh' for four years wrote an account that appeared in The Field magazine in 1874:

> SIR, - I have driven an Edinburgh for four years past, and under every conceivable variety of circumstances except an upset. My friends have once or twice contrived to upset my little trap; but to myself it has never happened, nor been near happening, neither with common care, need such a catastrophe ever occur. My tricycle weighs 83lb., and, when loaded for a summer journey of several days, it is made to carry myself (14st.) and an overcoat, spare clothes, a book, sketch book, colours, &c., to the extent of 25lb. This, as you say, is a good burden; but I do not find it necessary to be at all particular about a few pounds. I have always a comfortable seat to sketch from, or to rest in when I need, with great ease in driving. You may think it hard to move such a weight as I have mentioned. Given a good road, it is not so, even up a moderate slope, but I admit that a deep road will always beat me. In such a case, and in the ascent and descent of dangerously steep hills, I get out, and make use of a light line, the ends of which are fast to the extremities of the fore axle, and by which the vehicle is effectually and easily controlled both up and down hill. For easier stowage in a railway van, I have my driving wheel of 36in. only, therefor the speed is low. Although I can put it along on level ground at the rate of eight or nine miles an hour, I seldom cover more than six in travelling; but the road must be very bad to reduce me to four. This would not content many, but it is quite sufficient for my purpose, and to me far more enjoyable than racing over the country at fabulous speed. For locomotion only, there cannot be a question that the bicycle is best; but enjoying, as I do, a sketch from nature and a good book, and objecting to the scanty apparel I sometimes see on bicyclists, I am more than satisfied with things as they are.

This extract gives a good account of the sort of use that these machines were put to. One can almost visualise this old gent taking his tricycle by train to a rural station and then riding off into the country for a couple of days of peaceful sketching and reading. There must have been many who were awakening to the advantage of a machine which could be run for free and which needed the minimum of looking after, yet gave complete freedom to travel.

When the 'Edinburgh Tricycle' was first introduced about 1865 there was no real alternative to this type of machine. However, the time was right for the next evolution in personal transport, the pedal bicycle. When Matthew Brown placed adverts in The Scotsman newspaper in 1869 he was doing so in response to the threat of the new two-wheeler. The first advertisements for these imported machines appeared in February 1869 and then, alongside Brown's advertisement on the 3 April that year, was one for 'Elegant Parisian Bicycles'. A new era was about to begin.

Boneshakers and blacksmiths

The discovery that created the pedal cycle occurred in Paris. Most people accept this, but little else, as a fact. Exactly who first realised that it was possible to put cranks directly onto the front wheel of the old hobbyhorse is open to dispute. And, as with the Kirkpatrick Macmillan tale, the exact time when this occurred is not clear either. The two front runners, Pierre Michaux (possibly with help from his son Ernest) and Pierre Lallement, both lived in Paris, and thus at least, the location of this great development is certain. Lallement moved to the USA for a short time where he patented a front-wheel driven velocipede in 1866 before returning to France. There he set out to compete with the Michaux family who in the meantime had built up their velocipede business in Paris. Suddenly the two-wheel velocipede was big business.

Michaux exhibited his machine at the Paris Exhibition in 1867 and, at a time when people were embracing any new idea that came along, the craze for the velocipede exploded throughout Europe and the USA. Riding schools sprang up everywhere and the new toy began to be taken seriously in a way that the hobbyhorse craze never had. Reports of the new French velocipede rapidly began to appear in the British press. While a few isolated machines were probably brought back to England in 1868 it was not until 1869 that the craze finally crossed the English Channel.

The first evidence of velocipedes reaching Scotland can be found in an advert placed by an Edinburgh firm in The Scotsman on the 17 February 1869 : 'VELOCIPEDE (Paris Made) very suitable for Young Peoples Exercise - James Soutter and Son Importers 102 Princes Street'. This was followed a few days later by another advertisement offering: 'VELOCIPEDES! Velocipedes!! Velocipedes!!! Of the most Approved French and American Designs will Shortly be on sale and Hire at ROYAL PATENT GYMNASIUM at Moderate Prices'.

Soon after these imported machines went on sale various firms and individuals in Scotland were producing copies. In Glasgow the firm of T & F Smith in Great Clyde Street were making billiard tables and perambulators. Their workforce must have had the necessary wood and metalworking skills to build velocipedes and they grasped the opportunity. The 'Excelsior' machine that they built was advertised in an 1869 book on velocipede riding, suggesting that they were probably geared up to building the machines in quantity. Some other firms that advertised their machines in local papers and trade directories were obviously building more than just the occasional example. Banks Brothers in King Street, Stirling was such a firm and in Glasgow there were at least three other firms claiming to manufacture their own machines.

Other than T&F Smith there is no real evidence that any big velocipede business ever became established in Scotland. Glasgow was a major industrial centre and yet none of the velocipede builders were large enough to survive the short-lived boom. Equivalent English cities, such as Coventry, soon established a bicycle industry that was to continue right through the high-bicycle era and on to the present day.

However there was still plenty of money to be made from velocipede sales, hire and teaching. Indoor and outdoor tracks and schools began to appear to cater for the new fad. Widely advertised at the time, the Royal Patent Gymnasium in Edinburgh's Royal Crescent soon had the people of Edinburgh learning to ride. This was something that demanded entirely new skills, as few people would ever have had the need to balance themselves while sitting down and moving their legs. Equally difficult was the skill of steering the front wheel while muddy and rutted roads tried to redirect it in a random fashion. One further difficulty would be encountered when the rider tried to pedal hard as this had the effect of pushing the front wheel to each side alternately.

One of the earliest converts to velocipede riding in Scotland was William Flint of Edinburgh. His first machine had been a quadricycle that he is said to have ridden in 1868. This was described as being a huge machine driven by chain, rather than the more usual levers and rods of the period. He then became one of the first owners of a French velocipede in Edinburgh which he demonstrated on Princes Street in 1869. His actual machine was a 'Parisienne', built by Michaux & Co, and it still exists in the collections of the National Museums of Scotland, having been presented by Mr Flint in 1910. The quality of the Michaux is obvious even today, 130 years later. The paintwork is a deep red with black and yellow striping and the standard must have been comparable to the coaches of the day. The metalwork too is excellent with elegant curves and nice detailing, such as

A busy scene outside Glenalmond College in Perthshire with the arrival of a 'boneshaker' velocipede about 1869.

the acorn-shaped weights that kept the pedals the right way up. Few of the copies built in this country came even close to this quality.

One of Flint's first real runs took him Peebles, some twenty-five miles south of Edinburgh. He is said to have arrived there 'dead tired and sore' and been greeted by 'open-mouthed natives'. It is not recorded how he returned home but Peebles did have a railway station, which may have influenced his choice of destination for his first run.

Almost as soon as velocipedes became popular people started to race them. As early as 25 September 1869, just months after the first machines had begun to appear, an advertisement appeared in the Edinburgh Evening Courant for a velocipede tournament. The match was due to take place at the Royal Gymnasium in Edinburgh and was billed as a five mile race between Mr Keamoth of London and Mr Bathgate, the gymnasium instructor. No doubt the novelty of events such as this drew in the crowds and was good for the business of selling riding lessons.

One of the stranger aspects of cycle sport at this time was tilting at the ring which involved catching a ring on a pole while riding by, much as had been done by medieval knights on horseback. This was a sport that encouraged accurate velocipede riding and good balance. Flint won his first 'tilting' medal at the Royal Gymnasium in Edinburgh in 1872. He went on to become almost unbeatable at this sport, which was as short-lived as the velocipedes themselves.

Although there was almost certainly never a large industry building velocipedes in Scotland, they were being built in small quantities all round the country. In many cases it was blacksmiths who branched out into cycle building as the construction lent itself to basic blacksmithing. The frames were wrought iron and the saddle mounted on a flat steel bar, which acted as rudimentary springing for the rider. Although the machines acquired the nickname of 'boneshakers' this springing did make for a reasonably comfortable ride. The period of popularity for the wooden-wheeled velocipede was short-lived. The next development, the high bicycle, was not so easy to copy, with wire-spoke wheels and a large frame that needed real engineering skill to keep the weight down. This led to boneshaker copies being built well into the era of the 'penny farthing' high bicycle, and even, in a few cases, as late as the 1880s.

Typical of these blacksmiths was Adam Purves of Galashiels, in the Scottish Borders. Like many local smiths Purves was also an engineer and farrier and would have been interested in most new mechanical devices. Even deep in the rural Border country he would have been aware of the velocipedes from newspaper stories and possibly even from visits of intrepid bicyclists such as Mr Flint. Adam Purves built a velocipede about in 1875 but it is not known whether he went on to produce and sell them. Certainly a machine has survived and is still owned by his descendants in the town. A turn-of-the-century photograph of the Purves blacksmith shop in Damside, Galashiels, shows that he was running a cycle business by then. The presence of a horse along with a couple of bicycles tends to suggest that the cycle trade in the Scottish Borders was not lucrative enough to support itself.

Like many of the early pioneers of the bicycle trade in Scotland, Purves took an interest in the first motor cars and his business soon turned to this new, more profitable business with a garage in Market Street. Adam Purves & Son is still a thriving business in the town today and although the cycle side of the firm has long since been separated, the survival of the original boneshaker provides a direct link between the early cycle trade and today's motor dealers.

A surprising number of blacksmiths built machines that survive today, covering a wide geographical spread of manufacture and use. Their survival can only be put down to the fact that the machines were useless for anything other than what they were built for. There was also little scope for modernising or improving them as the bicycle design changed so dramatically during this period. The boneshaker very soon became a quaint curiosity compared to the machines that followed.

Examples of two blacksmith machines can be seen in the Museum of Transport in Glasgow. One was built by an unknown maker in Glasgow and the other by James Gray, blacksmith and wright, from Milton of

Mr T Fairbairn with the attractively carved velocipede that he built while studying engineering at Edinburgh University from 1867-1870.

This 1908 photograph shows Mr James Gray (with hand on his grandson's head) of Milton of Campsie near Glasgow with the machine that he is said to have built in 1865 or 1866.

Campsie to the north-east of Glasgow. Hawick Museum has on display an example built by Tommy Thomson of Stobs near Hawick.

Davis Low, an engineer of Losset, Alyth, built a machine which is now in the collections of Dundee Museums. This machine is unusual in that not only did Low produce a working drawing before he started construction but that this also survives today. Low is said to have produced his drawing after having seen a French-built example.

There is little evidence as to who exactly bought these locally-built machines. One exception must be that of a velocipede built in the town of Biggar. Here the local engineer was James Watt, a particularly talented man who constructed a huge waterwheel for John Blackwood Murray, father of the founder of the Albion Car Company. Watt had his own foundry and produced his own design of carts. One of these was shown in

26

the Great Exhibition at Crystal Palace in 1851. The evidence for his having built at least one velocipede comes in the form of a receipt that survives in the collections of Biggar Museum. The receipt shows that the town's chemist, Aaron Whitfield, paid the substantial sum of £6 to have a machine built. Perhaps surprisingly in a small town like Biggar, given that the receipt survives, the machine no longer exists. Even the interior of Whitfield's shop survives in the town as part of the Gladstone Court Museum.

Another type of business that lent itself to a sideline of velocipede building was that of the coachbuilder. The basic ingredients for a velocipede can be found in any coach; wooden wheels, spring steel and wrought iron. In Edinburgh the firm of Alexander Munro, in the Broughton Market, were advertising themselves by 1871 as 'Coachbuilder, Harness and Velocipede Maker'. They were even listed in the Post-Office Street Directory under the new category of Velocipede Makers.

Thinking back to the old hobbyhorse it is not surprising to find that the first maker in Britain was James Johnson, working at the heart of the London coachbuilding district of Long Acre. When the time was right for someone to add pedals to the equation we find that Michaux was also based in a coachbuilding district, this time in Paris.

Like the hobbyhorse of fifty years earlier, the craze for the velocipede among the fashionable lasted little more than a couple of years. However, while the hobbyhorse had led nowhere, the enthusiasm for velocipede riding spread, clubs were formed, and developments were inevitable. Again the development which revolutionised the two-wheeler came from Paris when M Meyer developed the wire-spoke wheel replacing the heavy, crude carriage wheel with something light and elegant. The only known way to gear up or down the pedalling rate was to change the size of the driven wheel and here was a completely new design of wheel, which would make this practicable.

This time round a different technology was required to develop and build these bicycles and the skills were not available in either the coachbuilding or blacksmith trades. The required connection had already been made when Rolly Turner brought back a Michaux to Coventry which was then copied and put into production by a business which was struggling in a very competitive industry. This industry was making the sewing machine.

High wheels and sewing machines

In Scotland there was one company that was ideally placed to enter the new business of bicycle making but it was not a Scottish company, at least not yet, and it made sewing machines. This company was the Howe Machine Co of Connecticut, USA. The idea of mechanical sewing machines had been around for a long time and it was clear that whoever perfected a device would revolutionise the textile industry and make themselves a fortune. The earliest sewing machine was probably that of Thomas Saint, a London cabinetmaker, in 1790 using the chain stitch principle. The real beginning of the sewing machine industry, however, came in 1846 when Elias Howe patented a lock stitch machine and proceeded to sell the patent rights. To understand how rapidly this business took off one need only look at the number of machines licensed annually by one of dozens of companies that rose from 800 in 1853 to over 50,000 in 1866.

Elias Howe made a fortune ($2million) from the royalties but it was not until 1867, the year in which he died and his patent expired, that his own firm 'The Howe Machine Co' started manufacturing machines. Everybody wanted one of these new miracle machines. Textile firms were revolutionised, and women at home could now make their own clothes faster than a professional seamstress had ever been able to. Demand was outstripping production and new factories were being built to cope.

Although there were a number of sewing machine companies in the UK the bulk of production remained in the United States and by 1870 there were seventy firms producing 700,000 machines annually. The larger of these firms found it more economical to set up subsidiary factories in Europe than to export completed machines. The Singer Company had established themselves in Glasgow in 1867 and this led the Howe Company to follow suit in 1872.

With Glasgow's concentration of engineering and heavy industry, labour and materials were cheap and shipping facilities to all parts of the world were excellent. Howe moved into temporary premises while a huge new factory was built in the Avenue Street area of Bridgeton near to

Schoolboys with their high bicycles outside Madras College, St Andrews. SLA

Singer's works. The imposing red-brick factory, designed by local architects Kennedy, Son & Myles, was built on American principles at the enormous cost of £15,000. Although equipped with American-made machine tools the entire works was powered by steam engines by Douglas & Grant of Kirkcaldy. The new factory opened in May 1873 and was soon making 1400 machines per week.

Here we find ourselves back with the story of bicycles again because almost as quickly as the sewing-machine boom got started the market became saturated. Howe followed the lead of a number of English firms and turned to the manufacture of bicycles in about 1880. This was a sensible move as much of the engineering applied to sewing machines was the same as that needed for cycle manufacture.

A reporter from a trade magazine who toured the factory in 1885 noted of the latest Howe bicycle that 'in its principle and construction are combined the best and latest ideas of general efficiency' and that it had been 'adjudged one of the lightest, fastest, and easiest running machines yet manufactured'. The reporter also noted that there was an average of 100 bicycles and tricycles being built each week by the 170 staff in that department.

Tricycles were clearly an important part of the production because, despite costing three times as much as the already expensive bicycles, they were popular with ladies. The social nicety of the time required ladies to wear tight corsets and long dresses which virtually precluded them from riding a high bicycle. Starley, in England, had experimented with a ladies side saddle high bicycle but had found it impractical and had added a third stabilising wheel. This became the Coventry Lever, and then Rotary tricycle and fed a burgeoning market for ladies' machines.

By 1886 the sewing machine industry was really in recession and the parent Howe Company in the USA went bankrupt leaving the factory in Bridgeton, Glasgow as an independent Scottish company. The bicycle and tricycle side of the business continued to grow with a thriving export

One of the medical staff at Perth Royal Infirmary posing with what looks like a brand new tricycle about 1882. The walking stick on his left suggests that the tricycle helped his mobility.

A sewing machine and a 'Scotch Express' tricycle both built by the Howe Machine Co of Glasgow and now in the collections of the National Museums of Scotland.

business. An office and depot was established in Paris, with a Scottish manager, which became a mainstay of the company business. Today the only surviving advertising posters are ones that were issued by the Paris office, and of the handful of surviving tricycles most were discovered in France. Not only had the original company been justified in diversifying into bicycle and tricycle making but also Glasgow's fine record for exports had clearly made it the right choice for location.

The fact that the company must have had a first-class sales department can be seen from their advertisements of the period. An advert in The Scottish Umpire in 1886 is headed 'SPEED WITH SECURITY' and declares that they are 'makers of the best bicycles and tricycles'. Even the choice of names for the various models of tricycle was inspiring with the Scotch Express, Flying Scotchman and Talisman front-steering tricycles, the Wizard tandem tricycle and the Spider and Albemarle high bicycles. At least three of these models have survived to be preserved in Scotland. The National Museum of Scotland's collections includes a Scotch Express and

a rear-steering tricycle while the Museum of Transport in Glasgow has an example of a Spider high bicycle. Howe was possibly the only Scottish company to have actually built high bicycles despite the claims of other smaller firms who probably only ever assembled machines from parts supplied by English makers.

One of the most plausible claimants was an Edinburgh cutler and surgical instrument maker, T E & R S Richardson. In 1881 they were advertising themselves as sole agents for Singer, Carver and another eight English makers. However, hidden among the small print they also claimed to be 'MAKERS of the Improved Edinburgh and Midlothian Bicycles'. A more likely explanation is that Richardson just bought in proprietary machines and badged them with their own brand, appealing to the loyalty of the local clientele. This practice became quite common with the next genera-

Tricycles were popular with women. Miss Mackay of Strathcarron is riding her Rudge 'Royal Crescent' about 1889. SLA

tion of bicycle sellers and survives to this day as a way of persuading people to support local business.

While doubt remains as to whether Howe were Scotland's sole maker of high bicycles, there do not seem to have been any other makers of tricycles at this time, probably due in part to the complexity of manufacture and also the high cost for small return. Tricycles remained popular throughout the high bicycle era due to the ease with which they could be ridden by ladies and by less athletic gentlemen. They would, however, always remain a small part of the cycle market.

While the 1870s and 80s may not have been a boom time for cycle manufacture in Scotland there was clearly a huge surge in interest in cycle touring and racing. Nowhere is this more apparent than in the number of clubs that were formed during this period. Probably the first to be formed in Scotland, and even possibly in the UK, was the Edinburgh Amateur Bicycle Club in March 1870, catering for the new velocipede craze. As was to become the norm in the Victorian era the club introduced its own distinctive uniform. The club colours were dark blue and red with the St Andrew's cross - what a fine sight the riders must have made riding their wooden-wheeled velocipedes in formation, being directed by the captain's bugle.

Other clubs were slow to form at first but as the new lightweight high bicycle began to gain popularity so too did club membership. At first it was simply a social thing for like-minded enthusiasts but it soon became part of a growing lobby fighting prejudice against this new form of independent travel. Many of these clubs were small local groups but others, such as the Cyclists

Mr William Flint in his garden at Portobello, Edinburgh, about 1890 with the New Rapid high bicycle that he presented to the National Museums of Scotland in 1910.

Touring Club, founded in 1878, were national in character. By this time clubs were being formed in every part of the country with the cities playing host to a wide variety catering for all interests and classes. Many of the club captains were prominent athletes or were becoming involved in the cycle trade.

In the 1870s the exploits of cyclists was still very newsworthy, at least in local newspapers. One report, in the Alloa Journal and Clackmannanshire Advertiser of 14 June 1879, is titled 'Long Bicycle Ride'. The article tells us that 'On Wednesday afternoon, about three o'clock, Mr David Melvin and Mr Robert Procter left Alloa on bicycles and that evening reached Balloch, a distance of 37 miles. Next morning they went up by

Loch Lomond to Crianlarich and from there to Lochearnhead, Callendar, etc. reaching Alloa about 8 o'clock on Thursday evening. The distance covered by the two gentlemen was 122 miles'. This was hardly a very long journey by later standards but interest in the activities of high-bicycle riders was huge at this time. One of the riders here, David Melvin, is interesting in a wider context as he went on to succeed his father John in the family cycle business in Alloa.

Probably the best account of the state of Scotland's roads about this time can be found in an account written in 1888 by Cdr C E Reade RN. Writing under the pseudonym of 'Nauticus' he describes a 2,446 mile (3,935km) tour which he undertook on his Cheylesmore tricycle in the summer of that year. Starting in Newcastle upon Tyne on 4 June the journey covered most of Scotland, reaching Wick in the north and ending in Penrith sixty-eight days later. After reaching Crieff on the twenty-sixth day Reade's companion, riding another tricycle, turned for home leaving him to ride the rest of the trip alone.

One of the most interesting comments that Reade has to make on the condition of the roads is that he found them 'decidedly bad' until he reached the Trossachs but that the next 750 miles through the Highlands were in 'splendid condition'. He notes that 'the Scotch mend their roads very skilfully, being careful to break up the stones well before laying them down'. One possible reason for the poor state of the roads in the South might have been the increase in tourist coaches generated by the spread of the railway system and Scotland's popularity with Queen Victoria.

In introducing his book Cdr Reade comments that 'Crowded coaches and tourists' grievances made me value more than ever the advantages of this enjoyable and independent way of travelling'. This sentiment is just as valid in the late twentieth century as it was in the nineteenth century and the freedom to enjoy Scotland's scenery by pedal power has remained popular in the intervening years.

Birth of the safety

While the high bicycle might have suited the energetic young enthusiasts, and the tricycle suited older people and ladies, neither provided the all round suitability necessary for the pedal-powered vehicle to become a universally accepted form of transport. The problem with the high bicycle was that it required a certain amount of athleticism to ride it and the method of mounting and bestriding it made it wholly unsuitable for ladies at that time. The tricycle, on the other hand, was easy to mount and could be ridden while wearing corsets and long dresses. However, the drawbacks to the tricycle were many and included the weight of the construction, the uncomfortable ride from three tracks, rather than one, along the rutted roads and the difficulty of providing storage for such a large object.

What was needed was a low machine that would have the facility to alter the gearing to suit the rider and terrain. The first attempts to produce such a design were simply the old high bicycles with lever drive. This developed into a slightly more practical machine with a short chain-driven geared drive that allowed a smaller front wheel. These machines became the first safety bicycles. The final development of the safety bicycle came with the understanding that it should be the rear, and not the front, wheel that should be driven. By about 1885 the first machines that we can recognise as the modern bicycle began to appear, produced by firms such as Rover and Humber. Here the bicycle had come almost full circle from the original hobbyhorse with nearly equal-sized wheels and a saddle height that allowed the rider to stand astride the machine. When the group of early Scottish innovators designed a treadle drive to the rear wheel they were very close to the modern cycle; if only they had substituted the treadle and rods with chain and sprockets, a form of drive which was used in coal mines at that time.

The small Scottish cycle industry responded to these design changes as fast as the market demanded them. The Howe Machine Co in Glasgow continued to produce tricycles but increasingly production moved over to the safety bicycle. In their 1888 catalogue they still listed four high bicycles including their old favourite the 'Spider', but there were also four rear-driving safety machines. The company was also still concentrating on tricycles at this stage with nine different models listed including the 'Witch', 'Talisman' and 'Record'.

The tricycles were probably still aimed at the female market with the 'Record' being listed as, 'The Ladies Tricycle', and the tandem version being sold as 'Well suited for two Ladies'. The catalogue illustrations, however, still showed male riders on all the machines, including the tricycles, and it would not be until the mid 1890s that ladies were almost fully accepted as cyclists or tricyclists. Certainly in 1888 ladies would have found little

A Scot far from home. Mr James Fleming in Italy during a tour of Europe about 1892, at the time that he was an apprentice architect in Glasgow.

encouragement from the catalogue to buy a bicycle, while at least on the tricycles Howe were offering leather dress guards as an option.

That the Howe bicycles were such a success was probably due in part to the quality of the machines and in part due to their advanced design. Many of the early safety bicycle designs left a lot to be desired and there were often serious component failures. Howe made a feature of their rear sprocket and the hub being forged as one piece to avoid the sprocket coming loose, apparently a common problem. No mention was made, however, of this arrangement requiring a new hub and wheel rebuild when the sprocket wore out.

As to the design of their safety bicycles they were almost always ahead of most other firms. In one magazine advertisement in 1889 this is graphically illustrated. Half of the page is taken up by an illustration of the Howe 'Speedwell' Safety. This shows a machine with straight frame tubes formed into the diamond shape intersected by the seat tube, the now familiar shape of the bicycle. The other half of the page illustrates the 'Swift' new light roadster, the latest offering from the one-time market leaders Coventry Machinist's Co. This bicycle still featured curved tubes and an open diamond without the seat tube.

The bicycle had almost come of age. Frames were now being built from hollow tubes formed into the diamond shape with that all-important intersecting seat tube across the points giving a strong, lightweight structure. The wire-spoke wheels were now roughly equal in size and the first designs for changeable gears were appearing. With the change in design came the first practical brakes that did not risk the rider coming a cropper over the handlebars. But for one last development we had a bicycle recognisable as the one that we know today. This last piece in the jigsaw was the pneumatic tyre. Up to this point tyres used on bicycles and tricycles were of solid rubber or, latterly, hollow rubber known as cushion tyres. The problem was that there was no elasticity in the solid tyre, giving an uncomfortable ride and poor grip, and too much elasticity in the cushion tyre, giving uncertain handling characteristics.

Horse drawn carriages, particularly those used in towns, had long been using similar solid tyres but perhaps the different circumstances of a sprung carriage, with no need for grip, had meant that there was little incentive for development here. However, experiments had been made by Robert Thompson of Stonehaven into fitting carriages with inflatable

The Erecting Shop in the attic space of the huge Howe factory in Bridgeton, Glasgow, as illustrated in the firm's 1893 sales brochure.

tyres to improve the ride; he patented the device in June 1846 and become the inventor of the pneumatic tyre. A number of Brougham carriages were fitted with Thompson's Aerial wheel, as he called it, and experiments were carried out in London to measure the force required to pull a carriage so equipped. The results that were published in The Mechanics Magazine in 1849 showed a reduction of 38% using a Macadam surfaced road and a mammoth 68% over newly laid broken flints.

Perhaps the invention might have been put into production at this time had the bicycle been at a more advanced stage of development but every invention has its time and there was insufficient interest from carriage makers to make this the time for the pneumatic tyre. Possibly problems with frequent punctures from horseshoe nails (a problem found later on by cyclists), and the difficulty of repairing the tyre, led to the idea being forgotten. Thompson died in 1873 without ever knowing what a contribution his invention would make to the development of transport.

It was left to another Scot, John Boyd Dunlop, to develop the pneumatic tyre quite independently in 1888. Dunlop was born in Dreghorn, Ayrshire on 5 February 1840. He studied Veterinary Medicine in Edinburgh and moved to Northern Ireland, eventually settling in Belfast where he set up a veterinary practice. Dunlop was a man obsessed with health and it was concerns for his ten-year-old son Johnny, riding his bone-jarring solid-tyred tricycle on the streets of Belfast, which led him to experiment with pneumatic tyres. It was not until later that Dunlop would discover that his idea was not an original one. His first experiments involved rolling a wooden disc fitted with a crude air-filled tyre along the yard at his house and comparing the distance travelled with that of a solid rubber-tyred wheel from Johnny's tricycle.

The results were astonishing with the solid tyre stopping before the end of the yard whereas the pneumatic one hit the wall at the end and bounced back along the yard. In February 1888 a pair of crude tyres were fitted to wooden rims and tested on Johnny's tricycle with encouraging results. Dunlop was now ready to make his first pair of proper tyres and fit them to a bicycle. Special wheels were required, as the rims currently in use would have been too narrow. A local Belfast cycle maker, Edlin & Co, was commissioned to make a pair with broad, gently curved rims. Finding a firm to make the tyres was more difficult and eventually Dunlop looked to his native Scotland for a manufacturer. The company he eventually commissioned was Thornton & Co, an India-rubber goods manufacturer in Princes Street, Edinburgh.

Even Thornton's was at first reluctant to take on the work, explaining to Dunlop that his idea was a fad, impracticable and that he was wasting his money. They were eventually persuaded that this was a serious proposition and the first pair of tyres were made in Edinburgh using finest Arbroath sailcloth covered in India-rubber. The result was a bicycle that was more comfortable and easier to propel than anything that had gone before. After twelve months and 3,000 miles of riding Dunlop removed the front wheel and cut open the tyre for inspection where it was found to be in excellent condition. Not one puncture had occurred during this time and the pneumatic bicycle tyre had been proven a success. This historic tyre and wheel were eventually presented, in 1910, to the Royal Scottish Museum (now the National Museums of Scotland) in Edinburgh, where it resides today. The rear wheel was sent to France as evidence during a patent application and was never seen again.

A patent on his new tyre was accepted in July 1888 and a new company, the Pneumatic Tyre and Booths Cycle Agency, was formed in 1889 to develop and market the tyre. The success of the tyre in racing ensured its commercial success almost as soon as it appeared on the market in 1890. At the annual cycle trades show, the Stanley Show, in London that year there were exhibited 1,543 cycles fitted with solid tyres and only twenty with the new pneumatic tyre. Four years later the situation had reversed with only three bicycles using solid tyres and 1,588 fitted with pneumatics.

The rapid success of the pneumatic tyre came about despite many manufacturers' initial caution. In the 1892 sales catalogue issued by the New Howe Machine Company they were very sure of the quality of the

A poster produced by the Howe Company office in Paris where much of their export business was done. The costumed lady suggests that the firm had aspirations to open up a new market in Spain.

solid and cushion tyres which they were fitting with a guarantee that any that proved to be defective within twelve months would be replaced.

However, when it came to offering pneumatic tyres New Howe were clearly being very cautious when they stated that 'Every care is exercised in the selection and fitting of Pneumatic Tyres, but our guarantee is only equal to that given by their respective makers, we shall, however, always endeavour to obtain the most liberal treatment for our Customers'. The cost of fitting pneumatics was also against the customer. With the New Howe 'Special' No 6 Roadster costing £15 as standard, fitted with the best solid tyres, the extra £5 to have Dunlop pneumatic tyres fitted was a huge premium to pay.

Against all the odds the Dunlop pneumatic tyre was immediately popular but the design had one major drawback. The construction of the tyre was such that it was effectively bound onto the rim with the sail canvas making it almost impossible to repair a puncture at the roadside. Although Dunlop's original tyres had covered 3000 miles without puncture this was perhaps more by luck than design. At this time the greatest hazard was not so much the sharp flints on the roads but more from the nails shed from horses' hooves.

A Scottish company, The North British Rubber Co of Edinburgh, provided a solution to the problem with a detachable tyre. The company had been founded in 1855 by an American, Henry Lee Norris, who saw advantages in manufacturing rubber products in Scotland with all the basic raw materials (except the rubber) being readily available. Premises were found at Castle Mills, a disused silk mill. Situated on the outskirts of central Edinburgh the location was ideal, with a canal and a railway passing by and the port of Leith only a short distance away. One of the first products was rubber footwear in the form of galoshes. In 1870 the company first became involved in road transport when they made solid rubber tyres for Robert Thomson to fit to his road steamers.

It was to be W E Bartlett, general manager of the company and son-in-law of the founder, who made the breakthrough in bicycle tyre design. In October 1890 he patented a detachable tyre known as the Bartlett-Clincher which used a beaded edge to grip a groove in the edge of the wheel rim. The original Dunlop design was immediately made redundant by the new detachable tyre. Another version, the wired-edge tyre was patented in England just days before Bartlett's design.

The introduction of the pneumatic tyre had come at the perfect time in the history of the bicycle with the diamond-shape frame having been perfected, usable brakes introduced and a riding position developed which suited the human body. Bicycles were now safe and easy to ride.

Club runs were now even more popular than in the days of the high bicycle and open to a much wider section of the population. On any given Saturday there would have been dozens of runs taking place. Looking at just one particular day in April 1891 there were twenty-six organised club runs from Edinburgh alone. The distance and style of these runs varied greatly from club to club. The Edinburgh Western was advertising a short route from Rutland Square in the centre of Edinburgh to Balerno, some eight miles away. On the other hand several, including the Merchison and Edinburgh Northern, were offering three-day tours.

Runs were often written up in the various cycling magazines including The Scottish Cyclist. Tranent in East Lothian seemed to be a popular destination and on one particular Saturday was visited by fourteen members of the Forth CC, and fifteen from the Edinburgh Eastern CC. The 'Forthites' apparently arrived first and took tea at the Crown Hotel so when the other club arrived they felt crowded out and turned for home, stopping for tea in Musselburgh. Most of the runs involved stops for tea but occasionally these stops developed into something more lively. Mr and Mrs Fraser, the owners of the Leadburn Inn, 20 miles south of Edinburgh, must have had their hands full when three clubs arrived at the same time. The tea stop then developed into a concert with one club member known as 'Jolliboi' distinguishing himself by his original songs.

Cycling was no longer the sole preserve of the enthusiast and the time was ripe for a cycling boom. A clear indication of acceptance of the bicycle into polite society can be found in the advertisement section of theatre programmes. At the end of 1893 a search through a programme for the Theatre Royal, Edinburgh would find a single advertisement, for Wood & Co of Cockburn Street selling Elswick Cycles. By 1895 five adverts could be found and this was typical for the remaining years of the nineteenth century.

One of the advertisements in 1895 was for Walter Hislop's cycle depot in Castle Terrace, Edinburgh. Hislop had been in business since 1880 and had survived some difficult years to take advantage of the new sales boom. It is clear in his advertisement from which area of society his new

One of the many riding schools that sprang up in the 1890s was that of Walter Hislop, a well-known Edinburgh cycle dealer. The hall, at Forrest Road, is almost unchanged today.

customers were being found when it states that 'Walter Hislop, Edinburgh, reports excellent business since the season opened. His society trade is increasing, and quite a number of titled notables, both ladies and gentlemen, have lately ordered safeties from him'.

The selling of cycles was only part of the cycle business at this time with the 'stabling' of cycles and riding lessons forming a lucrative side to the trade. In Hislop's advertisement he goes on to state that he has, during the current season 'taught upwards of 300 pupils (chiefly ladies) the art of safety riding on his commodious indoor track'. Among the machines being sold were 'Psychos' and 'Swifts' for ladies, girls and youths. A Swift gent's machine with Hislop's shop transfer on the spine survives in the collections of the National Museums of Scotland, an early example of a form of advertising which continues today with sales stickers in the rear window of cars.

Another advertisement in the same theatre programme is that for Thomas Calder of Haymarket, Edinburgh. Calder too was an agent for many of the top English makers but also claims to be a maker himself with the Calder 'Clifton' named after the shop location in Clifton Terrace. Here also the ladies' market is targeted with a ladies' 'Clifton' being offered at only '£12-12s Value unbeatable'.

The Nondescripts Winter Cycling Club members gathered in March 1893 to have their club photograph taken at Craigleith Quarry, Edinburgh.

Most cycle agents at this time seem to have offered their own brand and it is now almost impossible to determine whether these were bought-in machines which had the local name applied or if indeed they were being made on the premises. Other Edinburgh examples of the time were the 'Hanover' from Dunlop, Lawson & Co of Hanover Street, the 'Lothian' from the Lothians Cycle Depot in Lothian Road and the 'Dunedin' (after Edinburgh) from Rutherford at Canonmills.

Occasionally, a local make would attain fame beyond its humble origins. The Kalac, made in Forfar, became famous because of the exploits of the builder, John Killacky, a well-known cycle racer in the 1890s. Built using the unusual design of twin crossed over down tubes his own racing machine was a mobile advertisement for the firm. Another unusual feature of the firm was the issue of its own catalogue listing a variety of different models on offer. Such was the size of the firm that in addition to the factory in Chapel Street they had a shop in Castle Street and a branch in Dundee. What is even more unusual is that Forfar was also home to another cycle maker, Ballingal's, though it is less certain that they actually built bicycles on the premises.

The 13th Spring Meet of Edinburgh Cycle clubs in April 1899 saw over 600 cyclists gather in the grounds of the Edinburgh Burgess Golfing Society at Barnton. A large number of lady cyclists were present.

In contrast to the cosy social atmosphere and quaint locally named bicycles of home there was also adventure to be had from bicycling during the 1890s. One man took this chance for adventure to the extreme and cycled round the world. He was John Foster Fraser, a twenty-eight-year-old Edinburgh-born journalist, and he set off with two companions in July 1896 to undertake the longest cycle ride ever attempted. Over two years later after riding 19,237 miles through seventeen countries they completed the journey without any major mishap. Fraser wrote a book about the journey titled Round the World on a Wheel which was published in 1899 by the well known Edinburgh publishing and printing firm Thomas Nelson & Sons. Cycling round the world was one of the last great adventures possible at that time and if any further proof was needed as to the viability of the bicycle for leisure transport then here it was. The bicycle had fully come of age.

Bicycle transport

The early years of the twentieth century saw the birth of a number of firms that would play significant roles in the Scottish cycle industry in the coming years. The bicycle was no longer solely a novelty for the affluent or an enthusiast's plaything. Many working men now saw the possibility of using the bicycle for transport to work and this led many firms to start building cheaper models for this market.

Cycle shops began to appear in almost every Scottish town of any size, and many villages also. From the 'Zetland', of Lerwick, Shetland in the north to the 'Lochryan' of Stranraer in the south. From 'Victoria' of Glasgow in the west to the 'Bell Rock' built in St Andrews in the east. The first decade of the century saw literally dozens of new shops opening, many with their own brand of machine. Typical of these new shops was that which David Rattray opened in Glasgow in October 1900. This was to be one of the firms that would outlast most others and play an important role later on. Rattray was a twenty-two-year-old former ships engineer from Perthshire who saw an opportunity and took it. With help from his sister, Agnes, he opened a shop in McCausland Street, Glasgow, hiring out bicycles at one penny an hour.

Rattray was clearly a shrewd businessman as can be seen from an early Hire Agreement card that includes the following terms for the hirer 'To accept the Bicycle without any warranty as to its state, quality, or fitness for any purpose'. However, as if it were not enough that the hirer had to accept whatever he was given, regardless of its condition, he would also have to 'pay the cost of repairing or replacing any damage or loss that may happen to the Bicycle while I have it on hire'. Despite, or perhaps because of the rigorous conditions attached to his hire agreements David Rattray's business began to flourish and by 1903 the takings for the year amounted to £310 10s, a reasonable sum for the time. By 1913 the firm had outgrown the old premises and a move was made to 11 Murray Street, off Parliamentary Road. Rattrays remained at this address until 1968, making the shop one of the most enduring landmarks in Scottish cycling.

Mr Reid, the sciences master at Glenalmond College, Perthshire, after a week-long cycling tour with his wife, Easter 1901.

While the business of David Rattray grew to become arguably the best-known cycle shop in Scotland it was another Glasgow firm, Argyle, that became the biggest manufacturer. Founded in 1906, as the Glasgow Cycle Company, the firm set out to become a major industrial concern. Right from the start the company realised that to remain profitable through the quiet winter months they had to build up a strong export business as Howe had done before them. From their factory in Commerce Street, Glasgow, the firm sent salesmen to Africa, India and South America. The first large order to be received was for 2000 frame sets for South Africa. The robust nature of their export cycles gave the company an excellent reputation that ensured that the bulk of their production would always go abroad.

Cycle racing remained as popular as ever at the turn of the century with many great names such as Jock Miller and Jimmy Alexander at their peak in this period. Many cycle races were even included in athletics meetings and school games. But not all cycle events at this time were serious affairs. At the Glasgow International Exhibition held in June 1901 a group of cycling clubs got together to hold a gymkhana. The clubs involved included the Civil Service Cycling Club and the Glasgow Ladies Cycling Club. Perhaps the Civil Servants were encouraged to let their hair down due to the involvement of the ladies, but whatever the reason this was clearly a light-hearted event. In the introduction to the evening's programme the meaning of the word 'gymkhana' is discussed and it is decided that for this event it is 'an evening party al fresco'. The introduction goes on to say that 'The chief charm of the Gymkhana is the complete contrast it offers to the usual routine of sports meetings, a change which is rendered possible, and indeed necessary, by the presence of ladies among the competitors'.

That the event should be in complete contrast to normal sports meetings was almost an understatement. The evening got underway with a parade of decorated bicycles by the ladies, all unmarried except one, of the Windsor and Glasgow Ladies clubs. The winner received a silver brush and comb. Parades of decorated cycles were not new and could be found as part of fairs and picnics of all types. However, as the evening went on the events became more unusual. Event 5 was a Letter-Writing Race for ladies and gentlemen. The lady had to ride to her waiting partner who gave her a letter to read and reply to before riding back to the finish. First back won a brush and comb set, providing the answer to the letter was satisfactory.

The evening was working up to a bizarre climax with a 'Cigar and Umbrella Race'. This involved a complicated series of tasks with the lady giving the gentleman a cigar, which she had to light, and an umbrella to open, while he gives her an addition sum to calculate. Both had to ride back with open umbrella, lit cigar and correct addition sum all on the same bicycle. In the last race the lady and gent rode separately to 'Gretna Green' where they had to sign their names and ride hand in hand to the finish. Presumably evenings like this led to many real happy marriages of cycling couples. In contrast to these strange-goings on the printed programme ended by advertising the Scottish Cycling Union Championship races, a major event in the racing calendar, to be held a few days later.

One of the contributing factors to the strength of Scottish cycling at this time was again the quality of the roads. Earlier on we heard about

A group of cyclists on a run to the Ronachan Inn at Clachan, on the Kintyre peninsula, about 1900. SLA

'Nauticus' on his tricycle tour of Scotland and how he found that the roads improved as he travelled north. This was obviously not unique to the 1880s as an article written by the Victoria Cycle Co Ltd in 1904 expounds the virtues of Scottish roads. The article, entitled 'Cycling in Scotland' talks about the huge increase in cycling in the late 1890s and attributes this to 'the almost uniform excellence of the roads throughout the country'. In an article clearly intended to stimulate interest in buying a bicycle the writer tells us:

> Not only throughout the lowland districts, but in the Highlands as well, the roads are, generally speaking, excellent as to surface, while on all main roads the gradients are much less steep than might be expected from the contour of the country. ...The consequence is that not only does the Scottish cyclist enjoy facilities for cycling that are equalled in few European countries, but the fine scenery and good roads bring riders from England and places abroad in yearly increasing numbers.

At the time of writing this article the Victoria Company was growing fast, building not only bicycles but also motor bicycles. From their factory in

VICTORIA CYCLE COMPANY, LIMITED.

Dennistoun, GLASGOW.

Largest Manufacturers in SCOTLAND of MOTOR and other BICYCLES.

Factors for all CYCLES & MOTOR ACCESSORIES.

TRADE TERMS ON APPLICATION.

Elderly Beginner - "Grip her heid
ye nickerin' fule, or she'll pe aff"

*A humorous postcard sent in 1905 by an Aberdeenshire cyclist who writes that they are
learning their lessons on 'old Jane'.* SLA

Dennistoun, Glasgow, they declared themselves to be the 'largest manufacturer in Scotland of motor and other bicycles'. For many years their
chief rival was the New Howe Machine Company but they went out of
business in 1903 closing their colossal Bridgeton factory. Their demise was
caused by a combination of factors including the virtual collapse of the
sewing-machine business and too many cheap alternatives to their quality
cycles.

One of their smaller competitors was the firm of Melvin, in Alloa,
about whom we heard earlier. Sadly this firm did not last much beyond
Howe but for an altogether more tragic reason. By 1906 the Melvin
'Champion' cycles were 'well and favourably known all over Scotland'
and David, son of the founder John Melvin, was now running the
company. David had been an enthusiastic member of the Clackmannanshire Bicycle Club and a professional racing cyclist. However, tragedy

*A 1903 advertisement for the Victoria Company illustrating how little difference there was
between the bicycles and motorcycles that they built at that time.*

51

Horse power delivers pedal power. The arrival of a batch of new bicycles at the Forgue Emporium in Aberdeenshire, probably from the railway station at Huntly. SLA

struck when David Melvin died at the relatively young age of forty-three. In addition to being an enthusiastic cyclist he was also a motorist and motorcyclist. One Saturday, in July 1906, he had been on a motorcycle run to Dundee and St Andrews when his machine broke down on the return journey at Rumbling Bridge. Here he borrowed a bicycle to complete the journey but he collapsed at Forestmill and had to be taken home. He thought that he had simply over exerted himself, but his condition became worse and he was taken to hospital for an operation where he died. This seems to have ended a flourishing business. Perhaps, had he survived, the firm might have gone on to rival that of David Rattray. One Melvin machine is known to survive today and it clearly shows the high quality of bicycle being built in this small Clackmannanshire town.

Just as one business came to an abrupt end another was being started in St Andrews, one of the towns through which David Melvin had passed on the fateful day in 1906. Here a youngster by the name of James Christie had just left school, taking a great interest in cycling and cycle repairs. Many of James' friends started bringing their machines to him for repair in the washhouse behind his mother's boarding house. At this time he was working for a local grocer but soon found that cycle repairing was becoming a full-time business.

James was fortunate at this time in finding an old plumber's workshop for rent in South Street, St Andrews, and he was joined by his brother Jack, who had recently returned from America, in starting the business of Christie Brothers. They immediately set about building their own machine which they called the 'Bell Rock' after the small island which can be seen from St Andrews on a clear day. The brothers bought lengths of tube, frame lugs and ready-built front forks. The tubes were cut to length, pinned together and placed in a brazing forge where molten brass was poured into the joints. Each joint was then hand-polished before being hand painted with enamel which was baked hard in an oven. The brothers built all their own wheels, using Dunlop rims into which they punched holes; these were laced with spokes which they had threaded using a thread-cutting machine.

Several 'Bell Rock' cycles were sold locally. One man, a Mr Eadie, from nearby Strathkinness bought a machine each for himself, his wife and his son. Like so many other small cycle makers the Christies went on to sell motorcycles, cars and even lorries. James' son Gordon continued the cycle business until he retired and sold the business in 1975. The cycle shop finally closed in 1995.

The Christie Brothers were typical of many such firms, such as Purves in Galashiels who we came across earlier, starting in the cycle business and moving on to cars. Occasionally, however, cars and cycles were built side by side right from the start. One such firm was the Caledonian Motor Car and Cycle Company in Aberdeen. Founded in 1899 at 265 Union Street they realised the potential for building cars with tubular chassis using the same manufacturing techniques as bicycle frames. The De Dion engined voiturettes that they built were of very simple construction suitable for a small independent company. Larger Daimler cars were occasionally built to special order. Unfortunately the company only survived, building cars and cycles, until 1906. An example of one of their cycles has survived in the collections of the National Museums of Scotland. If the impressive brass headbadge of this 'Caledonia Special' is anything to go by then the company had much greater aspirations than is indicated by their early demise.

Scottish island communities took to the bicycle almost as quickly as each new development emerged on the mainland. At least two boneshaker velocipedes survive on Orkney indicating a very early interest in cycles.

C&J Macdonald of Armadale displaying the range of machines that they stocked, from child's scooter to an adult racing bicycle.

Certainly there was a very real advantage to using a bicycle for transport in the Orkney Islands for the simple reason that a cycle was an easy vehicle to transport in even the smallest of boats. A horse makes a very difficult and unpredictable passenger and the early motor cars required a special turntable to be fitted to the small ferries.

Orkney has always had cycle shops and even today they can be found in remote locations such as Longhope on Hoy. Orkney, in keeping with other parts of Scotland, even had its own makes of bicycle. Before World War I Mr Tullock, who owned the Kirkwall Cycle and Motor Depot in Junction Road, was advertising his own brand. Like other local makers he gave his machines a local name, in this case 'St Magnus' (after the historical figure whose name was also given to Kirkwall's magnificent cathedral).

Tullock made great claims for his machine advertising it as the 'Best and cheapest in the market'. Perhaps, if he was referring to Orkney as the market, then his claims might have been correct. But comparing a locally-built bicycle to one from Victoria of Glasgow for example would have been unfair, unless of course Tullock was buying his frames from one of the larger makers. He certainly advertised himself as being an agent for Victoria along with large English makers such as Elswick of Newcastle, and Sparkbrooke of Coventry. One example of the 'St Magnus' survives in a Kirkwall motor dealer's showroom today, allowing a comparison to be made with survivors from other companies of this period. The bicycle is an unusual sprung-frame machine showing a certain amount of innovation on Mr Tullock's part, whether for designing the frame or for having 'imported' such a design to the island.

Orkney, however, was not the most northerly part of Scotland where cycles were being built. That honour goes to Shetland, a group of islands that are closer to Norway than to Edinburgh in terms of distance and possibly even of culture. The first of these builders was Gideon Anderson whose premises in Commercial Road, Lerwick, were contemporary with those of Tullock on Orkney. Again, like Tullock, Anderson ran a Cycle and Motor Depot combining the two forms of transport, which were so closely linked in the early days of the motor car.

Anderson called his bicycle the 'Zetland Princeps' (Shetland Prince) and although he did not try to claim that they were the best in the market he did advertise that 'They are made well, run well and wear well!!'. There is also a very real possibility that he actually built the bicycle frames himself and did not merely apply his own badge. In addition to selling tyres and hiring out bicycles he also advertised brazing, plating and stove-enamelling services, all of which would have been required by a firm that actually built cycles.

Health and freedom

In the years following the end of World War I a movement towards the healthy outdoor life began to grip the country, giving the bicycle a new lease of life. Various factors were responsible for this trend and the cycle makers soon grasped the opportunity and helped to promote the outdoor life. One company that was to make more than most from this new movement was the Glasgow firm of Rattray, of which we heard earlier, being founded in 1900. In the introduction to one of Rattray's 1930s catalogues they attempt to explain the phenomenon themselves when they state 'When that unpleasantness was over, the reaction urged young folks to the open-air life, and Cycling and Camping became very popular'. The 'unpleasantness' referred to was, of course, World War I.

The early 1920s saw the gradual development of a new breed of lightweight cycle to feed the desire for machines which were easier to ride for touring and more competitive in the cycle road-racing which grew alongside the touring. Continental makers were not slow to push their products in this country and Rattray were agents for one of the more popular, Selbach. English makers too were marketed in Scotland by firms like Rattray, making names such as Sun, Grubb and Sunbeam familiar to Scottish club riders.

Scottish marques producing lightweight cycles were rare in the early part of the 1920s though there were still many small cycle shops putting their own names to bought-in machines. In Edinburgh the birth of a first son to a cycle and motorcycle dealer, Jock Porter, gave rise to one such new make. When Porter named his son Gerrard he named his own-brand bicycle the New Gerrard; Porter assembled cycles under this name using bought-in components until the outbreak of World War II. One thing which made Porter stand out from the crowd among the small Scottish cycle firms was the fact that he also built his own-brand motorcycles. It was with motorcycles that he achieved real fame when he won TT races in the Isle of Man in 1923 and 1924 on New Gerrard machines. After this even the badge on his bicycles featured the image of a TT trophy. It seems a pity that he did not have the same interest in cycle racing to drive him to produce his own lightweight bicycle.

This photo of the Glasgow United CC includes several well-known cycle trade figures including Archie Baxter (third from right) and Jack Smith (above the 'LA' in Glasgow).

The Glasgow Cycle Company had been building worthy roadster cycles from 1906 and had grown into a large industrial company by the 1920s. Much of the company's production was for export to countries such as India, contributing to the concept of Glasgow being the 'Workshop to the Empire'. The Argyle cycles that they sold to the home market were, in the main, robust roadsters that sold well as reliable transport and even gained large orders from police forces such as Glasgow's own. The company, however, were not slow to realise the marketing advantages of having a 'sexy' racing model in the range and they produced some fine lightweight bicycles. One original example that survives today illustrates this well with a bright red frame and even red rubber tyres. How many Scots must have drooled over such a machine in a cycle-shop window while struggling to make their 'easy payments' on the roadster that took them to work each day?

The Argyle racer would have been an inspiration to customers who would then buy an Argyle roadster, associating the glamour with their mundane machine. David Rattray probably had a similar strategy in mind when he too started building lightweight cycles in 1928, using the name Scot cycles to instil a brand loyalty with the Scottish club rider. It is probably no coincidence that it was in that same year that Jack Smith, who had joined Rattrays in 1916, became David Rattray's junior partner.

Lottie Smith at Strathblane in February 1928. Dressed in typical 1920s cycling clothing Lottie is riding an early example of the Mixtie style of cycle frame.

Jack was a long-serving member of the Glasgow United Cycling Club and was well known as a racing cyclist, making him an ideal contact with the racing fraternity. Jack's wife, Lottie, was a member of the Glasgow Nightingale Cycling Club and was an enthusiastic touring rider. Between them they must have been great ambassadors for the new Scot cycle. The idea for building a lightweight cycle may even have been proposed by Jack.

People like Jack Smith were the backbone of cycling in Scotland at this time, being involved in the trade, sport and also cycling for recreation. The editor of Motor Cycle and Cycle Trader once asked David Rattray if he ever regretted not having children to continue the business in his name. His response made clear the high regard he had for his junior partner when he said that 'most people have their children and their successors thrust upon them - I picked my own, Jack Smith'. Jack and his wife Lottie were frequent visitors at the Alexandra Park Street home of David and his sister Agnes. They would often be asked for a meal after work on a Saturday evening, followed by a game of dominoes.

By the beginning of the 1930s the signs of the coming economic depression were beginning to show. There was now even more enthusiasm for

The great racing and record breaking cyclist, Marguerite Wilson, with her manager while collecting a new Scot bicycle from Jack Smith (left) at Rattray's shop in Glasgow.

cheap and healthy cycle holidays and the Scottish Youth Hostel Association was founded in 1931 following the introduction of Youth Hostels to England in the previous year. A chain of hostels round Scotland was soon opening to provide basic and cheap accommodation for those who could not otherwise afford to leave the cities.

The hostels were open to people of all ages, religions and backgrounds and many lifelong friendships were made through their camaraderie. The SYHA was also strongly non-political which often placed a great strain on the organisation. One such difficulty was whether to acknowledge the German Youth Hostel Association and grant it reciprocal terms. As early as 1934 the SYHA honorary secretary, Dr Alen (sic) Fothergill, resigned over the issue stating that this would be tantamount to acknowledging the Nazi Government. The SYHA refused to interfere in politics and accepted the German YHA with a reciprocal arrangement.

The industrialised West of Scotland had the greatest need for the new Youth Hostels and the area also provided the easiest access to the spectacular scenery of Argyll and the West Highlands. Many factory workers survived the week with the thought of escaping the drudgery of their working environment, and tenement home, for the clean air and beauty of the countryside each weekend. As the area was also the largest centre of population in Scotland, it is no wonder that this is where most of the new builders of lightweight cycles established themselves to cater for the new market. As fewer people could afford to buy expensive machines from the larger, established, makers this opened up opportunities for independent makers with low-cost overheads to produce a cheaper alternative. There were other advantages to the local maker, such as the buyer getting a frame custom-made to their specification and being able to fit whatever components they could afford.

A typical example of one such firm was E & S Worrall of Hamilton. Ernie and Stan Worrall were both enthusiastic cyclists and club members. Stan worked in the family chip shop while Ernie served his time as a painter, using his bicycle to get to work. When they decided to build a cycle for themselves in 1930 they ordered all the parts from a catalogue and brazed up the tubes in a shed behind the chip shop. Club members soon got to hear about the Worrall cycle and the brothers began to receive requests to build frames for other people.

At first Stan would build machines by day and work in the chip shop at night while Ernie continued as a painter by day and built bikes in the shed each evening after work. Business went well for the brothers and soon they were renting the upstairs part of a plumber's shop in Regent Street, Hamilton. They built their own stove to bake the enamel paint that Ernie skilfully applied to the frames using his experience in the paint trade. All the decorative lining on the frames was applied using narrow brushes with techniques learned for signwriting. In 1932 they opened their first shop, in Duke Street, and began selling other makes of cycle. A large part of their business was undertaking enamelling for some of the larger Glasgow firms, including Rattray. During the difficult times of the 1930s the cycle builders could not afford to turn away orders, even when they were working beyond capacity. As a result the Worralls would sometimes receive orders from some of the hard-pressed Glasgow makers such as McCulloch and Dale.

Although the different makers would work together during such difficult times the competition between them for sales was always fierce. Most of the makers would advertise in The Scottish Cyclist with each using their own strengths to sell their product. Malcolm Smith in Glasgow High Street would, for example, highlight the fact that his business had been established in 1891 and that he was an official repairer to the National Cyclists Union and Cyclist Touring Club. Smith's own make, the 'Nightingale' was sold using the motto 'Genuine Workmanship Consistent with Reasonable Prices'.

J & A Baxter at Anderston Cross, Glasgow, used a different technique to sell their own make of machine. They advertised that 'The 'Star' Lightweight is SCOTLAND'S OWN', despite the numerous other Scottish makes at this time that could make the same claim. They also highlighted their personal service and exclusivity, with the machines being built on the premises by John Hamilton as a one-man job. As a result of this 'only a limited number could be turned out each year'. However, at the same time (in 1931) they were claiming that over 400 were already on the road. Possibly they were comparing their output with that of large firms such as Argyle.

Although the 1930s were a difficult time in the Scottish cycle industry it had it's lighter moments also. A story that highlights this relates to Andy McNeil who, along with his brother John, built McNeil cycles in Govan Road, Glasgow. One Sunday Andy was in their basement workshop building a special short-wheelbase tandem that needed the seat tube to be bent to clear the rear wheel. The process required the tube to be filled with molten lead for a smooth bend. The only lead that Andy could find was an old water pipe running through the workshop. As the pipe did not seem to be used he cut through it, found it to be dry, and now had the lead to allow the tandem to be completed. When Andy arrived at the shop on the Monday morning he was confronted by a crowd of angry women, and a flooded basement. Only then did he discover that the pipe was the main feed to the public washhouse next door and the only reason that it had been dry was that the supply was turned off on a Sunday.

Many Scottish cycle shops were forced to open on a Sunday during the depression of the 1930s. One firm that resisted the pressure to open was Dales in Glasgow. Dale even went as far as to place a tongue in cheek advertisement in Scottish Cycling News saying that he did not open because he was too busy counting the week's takings.

The working hours were, nonetheless, long in the cycle trade at this time. Jack Potter, who joined Rattray in 1937, remembers working until 8pm each day and 9pm on a Saturday. Although the Saturday night was

This happy group in the 1930s are members of the Edinburgh Ladies Cycling Club seen here on the outskirts of the city on one of their weekly Sunday runs. SLA

the busiest time for sales of accessories, prior to Sunday runs, the Friday nights saw the largest gathering of cyclists. This was when club members would meet to decide where their Sunday run was going. One of the attractions of gathering at the Rattray shop was that Miss Agnes Rattray would bring out a tray of apple and orange slices to hand round.

One of the biggest outdoor cycling events in the late 1930s was the annual rally of the West of Scotland Cyclists' Defence Committee. Held at Cumnock in Ayrshire the rally was supported by members of all the Scottish clubs with the common desire to protect cyclists' rights. Prominent speakers from various national cycling organisations gave speeches and proposed resolutions while sports events offered entertainment. Three thousand cyclists attended the first Cumnock Rally held in August of 1938. While many of those cycled in each day there were nearly 400 camping on the town playing fields. The location was ideal being situated in a sheltered glen on the outskirts of the town with facilities including a swimming pool, which was said to be one of the finest open-air bathing places in Scotland.

Reg Shaw, who became secretary of the Cyclists Touring Club, addressing the first Cumnock Rally in 1938.

The event was always strongly supported by the people of Cumnock who warmly welcomed the cyclists each year. No doubt there was good trade for the local shopkeepers. At the 1938 rally the Saturday sports events in the pool were won mainly by local residents, many of whom would be members of the local swimming club that perhaps gave them an advantage over the cyclists. In the evening Bailie Scoular of the Town Council made a welcome speech in which he highlighted the council's interest in youth with the provision of the pool for the town. Along with the pool, which was opened in June 1936, there were three tennis courts, a putting green, a café and football, rugby and cricket pitches. While not every town provided such comprehensive facilities most would have been drawn into improving parks and sports areas as part of the health and fitness movement of the time.

The Sunday sports were all cycle related with presumably less likelihood of success for the locals. Events got underway with a cycle polo match and the Zenith Wheelers resoundingly beating Douglas CC by 11 to 0. Most of the races were held for their entertainment value rather than any

A typical scene at the annual Cumnock Rally.

serious competition. The Pushing Bicycle Backwards races and the Tandem Obstacle race must have provided many a laugh. The object of the Cinderella race was unexplained but, not surprisingly, required male/female couples. The inner-tube bursting required a guess of the number of pumps required and was won by Mr Graham of Cumnock at 600 pumps.

After hearing five speeches on a variety of subjects a resolution was passed which makes an interesting comparison with the attitudes of today's cyclists:

> That this meeting of Scots cyclists strongly disapproves of the proposals of the Transport Advisory Council to deprive cyclists of their existing rights on the public carriageways and to make the use of rear lights on cycles compulsory...This meeting is of the opinion that neither cycle paths nor rear lights would make any contribution to the reduction of road accidents but, on the contrary, would have the effect of increasing the dangers to all non-motoring road-users'.

How different things are today with organisations such as Sustrans campaigning successfully for a nationwide network of cycle paths and all

Long before the advent of the mountain bicycle Scottish cyclists took to the hills. Easter 1939 and Meredith Williamson of Edinburgh looks down Glen Callater while on a camping holiday.

parties in agreement about the reduction in road accidents which these off-road paths bring. That the meeting should also decry the compulsory use of rear lights is even more amazing. Today only the foolhardy would venture out after dark without lights and many people now carry fixed and flashing lights for added visibility.

Few of the cyclists attending the rally would be aware of just how soon the matter of cycle lights would resolve itself. Little more than a year later war was declared and air-raid precautions made the shielding of lights compulsory. Many cyclists injured during the blackout would come to realise the importance of being seen. A white painted flash on rear mudguards, already a legal requirement pre-war, did little to avoid being hit by a car also using masked lights.

Wartime

The outbreak of World War II in September 1939 had an immediate and profound effect on cycling in Scotland. Cycle racing stopped immediately and the touring cyclists who had camped and filled the Youth Hostels in the summer of that year now found themselves in the armed forces. Many would not return to enjoy the freedom of cycling after the war was over. Many of the well-known racing men of the 1930s died in the conflict. One of the great names in tricycle record-breaking pre-war was Albert Watson from Edinburgh. Among his achievements was the RRA Tricycle 50 record that he took in a time of two hours and forty seconds in 1936, beating the previous record by nearly nine minutes. He was also well known as a track cyclist and rode a short-wheelbase machine that was specially built for him by Ernie Worrall. Albert died while training with the RAF in Canada.

Many cyclists now found themselves riding for very different reasons. One Edinburgh cycle dealer found himself riding a folding paratrooper's bicycle in the army. In the RAF many found that cycling was the only way to get around the vast expanses of the new bomber airfields. Soon, with petrol rationing, bicycles were the only private transport available to most people.

The Alexander brothers of Edinburgh made newspaper headlines with the novel way that they found to travel around together. In 1943 they resurrected the triplet bicycle which, as mentioned earlier, Jimmy Alexander had used in 1897 for record-breaking. With rebuilt wheels to take modern tyres, and upturned handlebars for comfort, the brothers James, Alfred and Henry could be seen regularly on a Sunday morning heading for Barnton or Duddingston golf courses on the outskirts of Edinburgh. Golf must have been the only relaxation that the brothers got during the war, as their cycle, motorcycle and motor-vehicle businesses were kept very busy during these years. Along with companies such as North British Rubber the Alexander Group was one of the largest employers on war work in the Edinburgh area in every type of work, from cycle refurbishment to the manufacture of motorcycle frames.

The Civil Defence Messenger Service comprised mainly touring and racing cyclists. This parade in the centre of Dundee was for Civil Defence Day in November 1941 and included members of Dundee Thistle Road Club. SLA

Most of the small cycle makers in Scotland were forced to stop building bicycles and take on other engineering work vital to the war effort. Larger companies, such as Argyle, also built military cycles alongside fuse cases and shells. This war work ensured that many of the skilled frame-builders found themselves in a reserved occupation and were prevented from joining up even if they wanted to. This was to stand many of the cycle makers in good stead after the war as they retained their skilled men.

Rattray, who had specialised in lightweight cycles, were not called upon to build military bicycles and they did not produce a single machine during the war. This, however, did not mean that they were not busy. With a staff of about twenty and a well-equipped machine shop they received plenty of government contracts. One of the largest of these was for the pins used to build the temporary Bailey bridges. At the height of this contract they were turning out 2000 each week. Another big order was for parts used to suspend the doors on aircraft hangars.

The Worrall brothers, in Hamilton, found that their business was not large enough to get the sort of contract that Rattray was getting. Stan

The bicycle became essential transport during the war. Mrs Jean Lyon poses by Loch Eddy while serving with the Women's Timber Corps. SLA

Worrall found work at the Parkhead Forge in Glasgow where tank armour was made. This involved him in cycling there every day, however, as that was his only means of transport to work. Ernie continued to work in the cycle shop and undertook a lot of repair work, in particular on carrier cycles, many of which were used in large factories. He can remember building a handful of cycles during the war, all of which were adult roadsters. To get the material he needed a licence that gave him a quarterly steel allowance.

The McNeil brothers in Govan did manage to build a few lightweight machines during the war despite a serious shortage of good quality material. Skilled labour was in short supply in Glasgow at this time and Andy McNeil was sent to work as a welder in a Clydebank shipyard, a far cry from brazing cycle frames.

A Glasgow man, John McAulay, bought a McNeil Brothers frame while he was home on leave from the army in 1942. Surprisingly, considering material shortages, the frame was supplied with an all-chrome finish and cost him £7-13s-6d (£7.67). The cost of all the equipment put another £7 onto the value when he came to insure it. Even in wartime cycle theft was common. He was gently reminded of this when, in a 1945 renewal letter from his insurers, it was pointed out that 'as you are doubtless aware, thousands of cycles are stolen each year, but not one in a hundred is recovered, and it behoves every prudent cyclist to protect himself or herself against this ever-present risk'.

Some businesses simply closed for the duration of the war and never reopened. One of these firms was Baxters in Argyle Street, Glasgow. Pre-war they had built Baxter 'Star' cycles in addition to being agents for other makes. John Hamilton, who had married into the Baxter family, was running the business at the outbreak of war and he took the decision to close up because of the risk of being bombed out during the Clydebank blitz. Subsequently Rattray bought the business and the 'Star' brand name, and Hamilton worked as a frame builder for them.

Interestingly Baxters were not the only Scottish maker to use the 'Star' name on a bicycle. John Gair, whose business was in King Harald Street, Lerwick, built a machine called the 'Shetland Star' in the pre-war period, continuing the Shetland tradition of being home to the most northerly cycle builder in the country. Gair was still advertising his own make after World War II in addition to being an agent for 'all the leading makers'.

A few bicycles were built by the larger cycle companies for the civilian population but due to the shortage of material they were poorly finished. One lucky woman was given an Argyle ladies' cycle as a Christmas present in 1942. However, she soon had cause to question how lucky she was as, within weeks of receiving the bike, rust appeared and the paint started flaking. The pedals used wood rather than rubber blocks and the handlebar grips were made from cardboard which soon deteriorated once it had become wet.

One of the hardest products to get during the war years was rubber tyres. Companies such as the North British Rubber Co in Edinburgh were working flat out on military contracts, principally making lorry and aircraft tyres. Tyres for military cycles had a fairly low priority and production for civilian cycles was almost non-existent. Eighty percent of the wartime output from the factory was for the military. Other products being produced included gas masks, anti-gas boots and balloon fabric.

During the war years bicycles had become a necessity for thousands of Scots. Factories relied on workers coming from a wider area than in peacetime. Workers and members of the forces alike needed some relaxation and it was again the humble bicycle that enabled them to get to the dancehalls and cinemas. Many had good cause to be thankful for the bicycle during the dark years of World War II.

Post-war revival

As soon as the war was over there was a rush to buy new bicycles. Petrol rationing meant that the bicycle was still essential as transport and the rigours of the war left most people wanting holidays again. The easiest way was by bicycle travel. Despite the continuing shortage of material Rattrays managed to turn out over 400 of The Flying Scot machines in 1946. Business was booming and in 1947 they needed to build new premises to cope. The new building was erected on the existing Murray Street site in Glasgow making it necessary to demolish half and build half at a time to keep the business running. The expansion was well timed because takings for the year in 1948 amounted to over £31,000, compared to only £21,000 in 1946. Production of the famous 'The Flying Scot' bicycle reached its peak at this time with nearly 1000 being built annually.

1948 also saw the start of a thriving export business for the company. In January 1948 a batch of twenty-five of The Flying Scot cycles were dispatched to Georgetown, British Guiana. An emigrant Glaswegian who spotted a market for quality lightweight machines had placed the order. Despite their other commitments Rattrays managed to complete the order in just six weeks. A further single machine was dispatched at the same time to a customer in New York, USA.

A new product introduced by Jack Smith for the female market was the 'Queen of Scots', a Scot cycle using a Mixte style ladies' frame but built to the same high standards as the 'Flying Scot'. Jack's wife Lottie who received the first example in 1949 may have prompted this decision. One of the first real outings for her new machine would have been a family tour of Ireland in July 1950 with Jack, Lottie and son John all riding Scot machines. The ten-day trip covered 520 miles, starting in Dublin and taking in Wexford, Limerick and Galway Bay.

Another early customer for the new ladies' machine was the well-known racing cyclist Reg Harris who bought one for his wife. Harris actually visited Rattrays to collect the frame and meet the men who had built it, including the frame builder John Hamilton. The whole staff turned out to have their photograph taken with the great man at the hand-over. Even

Mr and Mrs Ernie Worrall with son Ernie on a Sunday run in 1945 near the village of Douglas. The tandem is their own make and is attached to a Watsonian sidecar.

Jack Smith's son John got the day off school and donned a brown worker's coat for the occasion. Sadly, during this time of great success for the firm David Rattray died on 28 November 1950 at the age of 72. By strange coincidence his sister Agnes, with whom he had built up the business in the early years, died on the exactly the same date two years later.

Rattrays was by no means the only Scottish cycle maker that was enjoying success in the post-war years. Many now regard the 1950s as a Golden Era in Scottish cycle building with at least a dozen firms producing bicycles in reasonable numbers using their own make of frames and many more beside putting their name to bought-in machines. Much of this popularity was due to the pre-war trend towards fresh air and fitness continuing after the conflict. There was also a new prosperity with more people having disposable income, yet small cars, such as the Mini, were not yet available at a price affordable by many people.

The largest cycle firm in Scotland at this time continued to be the old Glasgow Cycle Company, by now trading as Argyle Cycles, the name that they had always used for their bicycles. In contrast to Rattray which built about 750 to 1000 bicycles per year, Argyle were building this number each week during the 1950s and 1960s. The bulk of the production was still for the export business as it had been from the beginning of the company in 1906. Each market called for a different specification and standard of finish. India, for example, required heavily built machines that could carry about three times the weight of a home-market bicycle. Anyone who has ever seen an Indian trader carrying produce on his or her machine will understand this requirement. Different countries also called for their own particular methods of dispatch. The United States, for example, specified each bicycle to be packed in an individual carton while Brazil asked Argyle to pack six to a crate. East Africa, a major purchaser, received their bicycles in crates of twenty-five at a time.

Douglas and Ina Wilson of Edinburgh pause at Gretna Green, during a touring holiday while returning home from the army after demob in July 1947.

Although the export trade was important there was also a good local market. In Glasgow one of the largest outlets for Argyle bicycles was through Goldbergs department store. The broad range of machines being built meant that there was a bicycle suitable for everyone. An Ayrshire family, that was typical of many others, would always buy the company's products. While the daughter would get a new Argyle 'White Heather', the son would get a Waverley, built by Argyle, and the mother a traditional black roadster.

The company also built fine racing and touring bicycles though they never had the reputation for this type of machine that firms like Rattray, Robertson and McCulloch did. Their top of the range bicycle was branded as a Campbell of Argyle to differentiate it from the more mundane cycles, and was named after the owner of the company at this time. The C of A, as it was known, probably deserved a better reputation as it was built using Reynolds 531 frame tubing and the finest components.

A typical Saturday scene in 1951 outside Worrall's cycle shop in Hamilton as members of the Royal Albert, Larkhall and Hamilton clubs gather to discuss the Sunday's runs.

The problem was that Argyle were best known for sturdy roadsters while Rattray had built their reputation on touring and racing bicycles.

The factory was divided into sections with each working on the assembly line principle. For example, the wheel shop that built about 5000 wheels per week had one person lacing the spokes, another truing up and another buffing the ends of the spokes smooth. Many of those employed in this section were women who were found to have more nimble fingers than men for lacing the spokes through the hub into the rim. Clearly not all the wheel production was required for Argyle's own cycles and one of the largest customers for the wheels was the Ministry of Defence for military cycles.

The paint section was another area where a lot of women were employed, enamelling and gold-lining the frames after they had been dipped in a rust treatment tank. The frame-building department alone employed between thirty and forty staff under the gaffer Frank McCulloch. One of the more colourful characters here was a Polish worker by the name of Ziggy who only had one arm but was capable of undertaking almost any job in the company.

By the late 1960s the company was in recession and the lower floors of the factory were let to Scottish Adhesives Ltd. Unknown to Argyle this was to cause the final demise of the company when, in 1970, a fire in the adhesives factory virtually destroyed the building. The owner at that time bought the surviving stock, mostly wheels, and continued in business from his home for a short time before finally bringing to an end the great Argyle name.

The big trend in cycling post-war was the fashion for all things continental, and in particular Italian and French equipment. One man who was shrewd enough to judge the mood of the time was John Robertson from Glasgow. He opened a shop in Govan Road in 1950 under the name Paris-Sport, specialising in continental products and dealing exclusively in racing cycles. (This name should not, however, be confused with the Paris Galibier and other bikes built by the London maker Harry Rentch.)

John Robertson remembers being inspired by some of the great continental racing men such as Coppi and Bartali and this influenced his style of business. Initially all the frames which he sold were well-known English makes such as Hetchins and Bates, the only exception being the French-built Mercier. However, after discussing with one of his employees, John Kennedy the well-known road-racing man, what the racing fraternity really wanted in a frame, he decided he should be building his own.

A frame-builder by the name of Walter Jackson who had learned his trade in Belgium was employed and production started. The bike was called the Milano, giving it a continental style in keeping with the rest of the business. In 1954 a Milano frame cost £15-10s (£15-50p) and was suddenly what many of the top Scottish riders were using. In total about 1000 frames were built using Reynolds 531 tubing. A further 200 machines were built using extra lightweight lugs and these were called Robertson to differentiate them from the other bikes.

Robertson used several innovative sales tactics that included forming a Robertson Cycling Club and having Scotland's first independent road-racing man, John Storrie, riding under the Robertson banner. Another ploy was to buy large batches of Gnutti chainsets to have his name engraved on the cranks free by the maker. Everything that Robertson did was just

John Robertson (second from right) with members of his own racing team in the back of his shop in the Govan Road, Glasgow.

that little bit different, including occasionally using his own aircraft to make trips to collect parts from the continent. In addition to the main production of racing cycles Robertson can remember building the occasional oddity such as the extra small frame ordered for a Glasgow barber by the name of Johnnie Ionti. Three racing tandems were also built, one of which, a Milano, survives today in a Scottish collection of historic cycles.

Although the cycle industry in Scotland was never huge, and was not going to rival that of the English Midlands, there were other interests in the industry. One of the largest producers of cycle tyres was the North British Rubber Company in Edinburgh. Even before the advent of the pneumatic tyre the company had been in business producing solid rubber tyring. The firm might still have been making cycle tyres in Edinburgh today had it not been for a series of take-overs. A disastrous fire in January 1962 that destroyed much of the Castle Mills works added to the company's troubles. By the late 1950s over 70% of the firm was owned by US Rubber Incorporated and by 1966 a merger with Sto-Chem Ltd created Uniroyal Ltd, bringing to an end the company that had first produced the detachable pneumatic tyre.

Another ancillary cycle trade was that of H Miller & Co, an electrical firm based in the English Midlands. Along with many other industries in the early 1950s Miller's took advantage of cheap factories and plentiful labour in Scotland to open a factory making cycle dynamos at Newhouse near Glasgow. By 1953 business was so good that Phillips were also making these dynamos in their Hamilton, Lanarkshire, factory.

In a country that is famed for its engineering industry it is perhaps surprising that there were not more companies producing cycle components in Scotland.

There were other small firms involved in the cycle trade and one of these could be found in the unlikely situation of Hawick in the heart of the Scottish Borders textile industry. This company was B&T (Bantel) Ltd, a toy manufacturer that also made small cycle accessories such as mudguards, spanners and rear reflectors. The company had come to Hawick from London in 1969 and at the peak of their production in the 1970s employed a staff of 120. In addition to the cycle accessories they also made children's tricycles and scooters. Production of these only ended in 1996. This firm had even thought about starting a Scottish cycle museum. Their collection had been started when the firm was still in London and the bicycles were often used in events such as the Lord Mayor's Parade. By the time that Bantel purchased the collection belonging to the great Scottish racing cyclist Jock Miller in 1957 they had gathered about sixty historic cycles. Unfortunately the museum venture came to nothing and the collection was sold to a Canadian collector in 1972.

Another venture which was successful and for which the firm became well known was their professional cycle-racing team. Barry Brandon, one of the partners in the company, ran the Bantel team from the factory in Hawick. Barry was particularly good at spotting talent and many of the riders that he signed up went on to be very successful. Perhaps their best-known rider was Hugh Porter who won the World Pursuit Championships in 1972 while riding for Bantel. The company even made a few high quality

Schoolboys try out roller racing on the Rattray stand at the annual cycle show in the Kelvin Hall, Glasgow, sometime in the 1950s.

bicycles using the 'Hugh Porter' name. His name also appeared later on imported machines sold by Bantel. Both the team and the Bantel factory are now gone but the company lives on in the form of the Hawick Cycle Centre, and adjoining pram shop, which had always been the factory outlet shops.

Another unlikely location to find a company producing cyclists' requisites was Cellardyke in the East Neuk of Fife. Robert Watson and Co had been making oilskins for the many fishermen in the area since the 1860s. By the 1920s the firm had started selling lightweight oilskin capes, leggings and sou'westers to the growing band of club and touring cyclists of the time. The brand name chosen by Watsons for their cycling range was 'Cella' after the town where they were based. There were further factories in Newburgh and Buckhaven in Fife. Their advertisements pointed to the many benefits of buying 'Cella' clothing: they had a non-tacky finish, were light to carry and easy to fold. The firm served several generations of Scottish cyclists until the recession of the fishing industry and new waterproof materials caused the factories to close in about 1973.

One Scottish company producing cyclists' clothing today is Endura in Livingston, West Lothian. Utilising many of the latest fabrics they make shorts and tops specially printed for cycle-racing teams. Another speciality is waterproof jackets, though the bright colours and stylish designs bear little resemblance to the 'Cella' products of Watson & Co.

In the late 1960s there was a steady decline in bicycle sales and use. The small-wheeled Moulton, and its inferior rival the Raleigh RSW, had created a short revival in cycle sales through the 1960s which petered out as the fashion for all things 'mini' passed. This trend is reflected in the finances of Rattrays. After a drop in income in 1961 and 62 there was a sharp increase between 1963 and 1966 before things levelled off again for a few years.

During this period several well-known Scottish makes ceased to exist. These included Elrick of Stirling and Worrall of Hamilton. Some, like John Robertson, sold their remaining stock to Rattrays while others like Malcolm Smith sold their entire business. Smith had built his own machine called the 'Nightingale', after the club of the same name, and his premises in Glasgow High Street were kept on as a branch of Rattrays selling mainly Raleigh bicycles.

Rattray themselves were forced to move in from their Murray Street premises, which they had occupied since 1913, when a compulsory-purchase order was served as part of a clearance and regeneration scheme in 1968. After a short-term move to a former air-conditioning factory in Dalhousie Street, another compulsory move in 1972 took them to a more permanent address in the Alexandra Parade. Things seemed to go well for Rattray during 1972 with over 1000 Raleigh and Carlton bicycles being sold, more than any other Scottish dealer. By this time they had moved into the motorcycle market also, selling Yamaha and Puch machines to bolster what was overall a shrinking cycle market. The Flying Scot was still being built and about this time Billy Connolly, the Glaswegian comedian, had a Scot made for himself.

By this time the firm had become famous around the world and was frequently visited by Japanese, Canadian, American and European tourists. Often these visits would result in much needed export orders,

Billy Bilsland riding a Rattray Ventoux similar to the one he raced in the Mexico Olympic Games in 1968.

with The Flying Scot bicycles continuing Glasgow's reputation for engineering excellence round the world. Rattray bicycles even made their appearance in the 1966 British and Commonwealth Games in Jamaica. The Scottish cycling team comprising Albert McLelland, Jim Leach and Billy Bilsland all used The Flying Scot machines. In the 1968 Olympic Games in Mexico Billy Bilsland from Glasgow rode a Rattray Ventoux in the Road Race and Time Trial events. Later on Billy started his own cycle shop and employed a former Rattray frame-builder to build about 200 of his own-brand of bicycles.

Then, in February 1973, Rattrays were dealt a blow when Jack Smith died at the age of 69 leaving the business to be run by his wife Lottie and son John. Jack's funeral, at Glasgow Crematorium, was a tribute to the respect with which he was held both in the cycle trade and by the people of Glasgow. Well over 300 attended to pay their last respects to a man who had done so much for cycling in Scotland. Among those at the funeral were representatives from all the major companies in the trade including

The front shop of the Rattray Cycle Depot in Glasgow with a crate of Flying Scot bicycles ready to be dispatched to Hong Kong.

Dunlop, Raleigh, Reynolds Tubes, Argyle Cycles and Honda. Also represented were Glasgow Police, Glasgow City Corporation, Glasgow Rangers Football Club and the Scottish Cyclists Union. This was possibly the end of an era in more ways than just that of the death of a pillar of the Scottish cycle community.

Fewer people than ever before were using bicycles as transport and a new affluent society was using cars rather than bicycles for holidays and weekend trips. Gone were the pre-war days when there were hundreds of active cycle clubs in Scotland and the Youth Hostels were full each weekend with people escaping from the industrial cities of Glasgow and Dundee.

By the late 1970s cycle-building in Scotland was almost at an end and even Rattray & Co were producing less than fifty Scot cycles a year. In 1979 Jack Potter, the front-shop manager, retired and Steyr Daimler Puch purchased a 51% stake in the company to gain their own Glasgow outlet. This arrangement lasted a couple of years before the company was sold again, this time to Evan Ritchie who already owned a cycle shop in Aberdeen. Ritchie had great plans to revitalise the Scot name with a wider range of more affordable machines. Sadly Evan Ritchie's plans failed and a year later, in April 1983, Rattrays finally went into receivership. The shop stock along with the The Flying Scot name were bought by Jim Houston, owner of Dales (Cycles) Ltd in Glasgow and a long tradition of cycle building came to an end. Today in 1999 it is still possible to buy a bicycle called a Flying Scot but the frame will have been built in Newcastle-upon-Tyne.

Albert Moffat applying a Flying Scot transfer to a frame in November 1975. The gas lighting was installed to cope with electricity cuts during the prevailing power crisis.

The mountain bike boom

After a lean time in the cycle trade and a decline in the numbers of cyclists a revival was about to happen. In part this can be traced to an underlying global concern for the environment, the need for more healthy lifestyles and more recreation time than ever before. But to find the origins we have to look across the Atlantic to the United States. Without a catalyst the revival would probably not have happened, at least not at the speed with which it did. A parallel can be drawn with the boost to the cycle industry in the 1960s where the catalyst was Dr Moulton's small-wheel bicycle and the undercurrent which carried it along was the fashion for anything mini.

In the case of the mountain bike we can trace its development to a homespun sport in California and in particular to the Marin County area. Clunker or downhill racing involved taking an old heavily-built American cruiser bicycle, such as the Schwinn Phantom, and stripping it to the bare necessities. This would then be raced down a rough mountain track against other similar bikes. As the supply of suitable clunker bicycles began to dry up the next stage was to have machines specially built for the purpose. The first of these came from small custom frame builders in the San Francisco area in 1977 and by 1980 there were about 300 being built to a pattern which was beginning to resemble the mountain bike of today.

The first public airing for the new type of bicycle was at the 1981 New York cycle show. Here was a machine that had found its time and fulfilled a need much as the fashion bike of the 1960s, the health and freedom bike of the 1930s and the social tool of the 1890s. The rate at which the new fad for mountain biking took off can be seen by looking at the production figures. In 1982 the custom builders turned out 5,000 bikes in response to the previous year's show. By 1983 most of the big makers had woken up to the potential for this type of bicycle and 50,000 were built in the San Francisco area alone.

The cycle trade, like most other businesses today, is a global affair and almost as soon as the big players in the market got involved the mountain bike came to Britain. In Scotland the new bicycle was welcomed with open arms by the public and trade alike. The topography of Scotland was ideally

Mountain bike (ATB) racing at Penicuik near Edinburgh in 1990.

suited to a machine with fifteen and more gears and a riding position suited to hill-climbing rather than the head-down approach of most touring and racing bikes. Such was the impact of the new bike with large manufacturers, such as Raleigh in the UK, that there was never going to be a revival of the kind of industry which Scotland had supported in the 1930s and 1950s. For a start the last of the industrial-scale makers, Argyle, were no longer in business and of the small makers the most likely to have succeeded, Rattray, had closed its doors just a year before the boom hit Scotland.

However, although there was not going to be a revival of bicycle manufacturing there were plenty of firms ready to assemble and market the bikes. One of these firms which was ripe for the new market was a small worker co-operative in Edinburgh. The idea of a worker co-operative was not a new one but is more commonly found in the food industry. When the Edinburgh Bicycle Co-operative started in 1977 with a staff of three the word bicycle meant a road bike. By the mid 1980s customers would be buying so many of the new type of machine that the word bicycle would come to mean an All Terrain Bicycle (ATB).

By 1984 the business had expanded and was assembling its own brand of touring bicycles. As we have seen throughout the history of the Scottish cycle trade this local branding of bought-in frames was nothing new. However, this introduction to specifying and building their own brand was perfect experience for jumping into the mountain bike boom with their own machine, the Edinburgh Contour, in 1988.

Although the new bikes had a good Scottish name the frames were actually being built by M Steel of Newcastle. An example from this early

An Edinburgh Bicycle 'Contour' coping with the cobbles and hills of Edinburgh in the 1990s.

production can be found in the collections of the National Museums of Scotland, having been gifted by Edinburgh Bicycle Co-operative Ltd in 1988. Today the frames are still sourced from British firms such as Falcon, and the founding principle of a co-operative is still held, but the business is now a multi-million pound one with a staff of over fifty. At any one time there are about twenty full members of the Co-op with others on probation to join.

Although Edinburgh Bicycle is perhaps unique in Scotland for being a worker co-op it is not the only firm to be marketing their own brand of bicycle. In the West of Scotland, the heartland of the old cycle trade, there are several bicycle shops with their own brand. Milngavie Cycles produce the 'Highlander' in keeping with the tradition of a name that has a Scottish character to it and reflects the purpose for which it was designed.

While the original purpose of the mountain bike was to compete in sport, the mass sales could not have been achieved without a wider leisure market for people just wanting to get out onto the hills at weekends. Even this market might have been limited had people not started using the bikes as tough roadsters. Many people found the low gearing easier, albeit at walking pace, for the steep hills in many towns. The knobbly tyres were also found to give a more cushioned ride and be more resistant to punctures.

What had started as an ATB for the Scottish hills had now come to the city streets. The ideal machine would be a compromise between the ATB and the old style roadster machines. Soon hybrid 'city' cycles were being built. Edinburgh Bicycle Co-operative started selling their own-brand 'Connection' with the name reflecting the urban commuting for which it was intended. One of the most obvious changes was the fitment of mudguards, which on a full ATB would just have clogged with mud. Narrower, though still robust, tyres were the next stage.

The bicycle has come almost full circle with the city bicycle being no more than a modern version of the roadster that can be traced back to the first recognisable modern bicycle of about 1890. Current developments centre on the full off-road ATB. Lightweight suspension systems are now appearing on moderately priced machines, which only a few years ago were exclusive to top of the range models. Almost certainly this technology will, as it becomes cheaper, find its way onto the city bicycles.

Just as the balance of touring bikes to the ATB and its derivatives has changed, so too has cycle sport. This is perhaps even more pronounced in

Edinburgh 'Connection' city bicycles in an idyllic setting by the Union Canal just a short distance from Edinburgh's bustling city centre.

Scotland than in continental Europe where there is less of a widespread cycle-racing culture to change. Again the Scottish landscape has had an impact on the sport. Major off-road championship races are now held in places such as the Rothiemurchus estate near Aviemore where the forested hills reflect the nature of the origins of the sport in the USA.

However, despite the proliferation of off-road events every weekend, the traditional forms of cycle-racing have survived. None of the various types of cycle-racing in Scotland have ever been a big spectator sport though it has always attracted a large number of competitors. Just occasionally one rider stands out above all the others. In the 1980s the only rider to become virtually a household name in Scotland was Robert Millar. Glasgow-born Millar came up through the ranks of club and semi-professional racing in the 1970s but it was his performance in the Tour de France after he turned professional that was to make him famous. In 1983 at his first attempt Millar not only came fourteenth overall in the race but he also won a stage. Le Tour is known as one of the toughest in the world with an average of one third of the riders failing to finish. Among first-year riders the percentage is even higher.

Building on his success in 1983 Robert Millar went back in 1984 to achieve what was probably the best result of his career. Again he took a stage win, this time on the Guzet Neige stage, and finished fourth overall behind three of the greatest names in cycle racing, Laurent Fignon, Bernard Hinault and Greg Lemond. But it was his overall win in the King of the Mountains competition that will be best remembered. After the 'maillot jaune' of the overall winner it is the green jersey of the best sprinter and the polka-dot jersey of the King of the Mountains that are the most coveted awards in the Tour de France.

Millar continued racing in Le Tour each year until he retired at the end of 1993. But, although he achieved another stage win in 1989, and several very good finishes, it was the 1984 race, which marked him out among the great cycle-racers. His name is still well known on the continent. Throughout most of his career he lived abroad and this probably explains why, despite a loyal following in Scotland, he is not better known in the UK generally.

If Millar was the man of the 1980s then Graeme Obree had to be the name of the 1990s, and is probably even better known. Possibly what has made Obree such a celebrity was the way in which he seemed to come from nowhere to take the world one-hour record in 1993. What made the cycling world sit up and take notice was that the previous record holder was the internationally respected rider Francesco Moser. What caused the public to sit up and take notice was his unusual riding position and his home-built bicycle that used bearings from a washing machine. The fact that the bearings were ideal, due to their quality and low friction, and that his riding position helped his breathing was all lost on the press who only saw him as an eccentric.

The one-hour record is one of the longest running and most highly prized in cycling. First contested in 1876, when the record was set at 25.508 kilometres in an hour, the distance had risen to 51.151 kilometres when Moser took the record in 1984. When Obree beat this he was taking the record to near the limits of human ability. Despite his many other achieve-

Sarah Phillips from Stonehaven poses at the 1996 Olympic Games in Atlanta with the Glasgow-built 'Dave Walsh' machine that she raced.

ments during his racing career it will always be this record for which he is remembered, along with the fact that he built the bicycles himself.

Although the great days of Scottish cycle building are gone there are still a handful of frame builders left. Clarkston Cycle Centre in Glasgow has built about thirty bicycles to special order under the name of 'Dave Walsh'. Their frame builder Alex Cross, provides a link with the past as he served his apprenticeship at the Argyle factory and went on to build Flying Scot frames for Rattray. To see Alex working on a frame is like seeing a mirror of the past. The frame jig that he uses is the same as can be seen in old photographs of the Rattray workshop. The tubes, lugs and dropouts that he uses to build a frame are modern but the technique for brazing and aligning a frame have not changed for 100 years. Today many track and time-trial racing bicycles are made from carbon fibre and now aluminium is becoming popular for ATBs. But neither of these materials has yet provided a noticeable improvement on the traditional steel frame.

Probably the highest profile rider using a 'Dave Walsh' bicycle is Sarah Phillips from Stonehaven in Aberdeenshire. Sarah rode for Great Britain in the 1996 Olympic Games in Atlanta, USA, competing in the Road Race and Individual Time Trial. By doing so she was continuing the tradition of a Scottish rider on a Scottish bicycle, like Billy Bilsland in the 1968 games. The connection here is, of course, more than just superficial, with Alex Cross having built both Rattray and Dave Walsh frames.

Charles Ralph in Morayshire is today probably the only person in Scotland building bicycles in any reasonable numbers. His one-man business of Alves Frames near Elgin was started in 1985 and today he builds anything up to about fifty bicycles a year. He is also something of a rarity in as much as he also stove-enamels the frames on the premises, making this a true home-grown product.

Alves bicycles are a popular choice for Scottish racing cyclists and have been used by people like Roddy Riddel of Inverness to good effect. Sarah Phillips has also been successful using Alves bicycles in addition to her Dave Walsh machine. When Sarah rode for the Scottish team in the 1994 Commonwealth Games in Canada her choice of bicycle was an Alves. Many Scottish and British Championships have been won using Alves and the British twelve hour record was broken in 1998 with a bicycle from this small Scottish firm.

Gone are the many great cycle makers from the past such as Rattray and Argyle, but at least Scotland is still able to produce home-grown talent in cycle racing. How nice it would be to see the Scottish bicycles used by these riders enjoying the same success and once again being sold in their thousands the world over.

Appendix

Makes of bicycle and tricycle commercially built, assembled or badged in Scotland

Aero Bikes
10-16 Cluny drive
Edinburgh
1994-present day

Alexander & Co   *Wallace*
108-110 Lothian Road   *Alexander*
Edinburgh   *Alexander Imperial*

J B Allen
Jane Street
Leith
1930s

Alves Frames   *Alves*
Charles Ralph
Elgin Springs
Longmorn
Elgin
1985-present day

Gideon S Anderson   *Zetland Princeps*
Commercial Road
Lerwick
Shetland

K Anderson
52 Maitland Street
Glasgow

W D Annat   *Southern*
Southern Cycle Depot
25 Newington Road
Edinburgh
c1905

John Anthony
115 South Street
Armadale
West Lothian

R Ballingall   *Elite*
118 East High Street
Forfar
c1900-c1930

Bantel Ltd   *Hugh Porter*
Burnfield Industrial Estate
Hawick
1970s

J & A Baxter   *Star*
9 Washington Street
Anderston Cross
Glasgow

Billy Bilsland Cycles   *Billy Bilsland*
Glasgow

Boarhead   *Boarhead*
Glasgow

W Borthwick & Co   *Cameronian*
32-36 Cockburn Street
Edinburgh
1920s-1930s

James M Boyd   *Gala Waverley*
Waverley Cycle Works
Market Street
Galashiels
c1898-c1905

Caledonian Motor Car and Cycle Co
Special Caledonian
265 Union Street
Aberdeen
c1899-c1910

Thomas Calder   *Clifton*
9 Clifton Terrace
Edinburgh
1890s

Christie Brothers   *Bell Rock*
55 South Street
St Andrews
Fife

John Connel   *Wester Ross*
Aultbea
c1980-c1985

D C Cruikshank   *Orient*
13 Rosemount Viaduct
Aberdeen

A Dale   *Dale Bantam*
15 Shamrock Street
Glasgow

Dales (Cycles) Ltd   *Flying Scot*
150 Dobbies Loan
Glasgow
1980s-present day

Robert Davidson   *Gladstone*
354 King Street
Aberdeen
c1909

Dick Brothers
Edinburgh Road
Dalkeith
c1920

Jim Docherty
Lochwinnoch
Renfrewshire
Parkhead
Glasgow
1988-present day

Andrew Downie   *The Haymarket*
19-33 Haymarket Terrace
246 Morrison Street
Edinburgh

James Downie & Sons
Lochryan Cycle Works
Stranraer
1873-1900s

Dunlop, Lawson & Co   *Hanover*
38-40 Hanover Street
Edinburgh
1890s

The Economic Cycle &   *Lothian*
   Motor Co   *Lothian Royal*
42 Nicolson Street
Edinburgh
Early twentieth century

Edinburgh Bicycle   *Country*
   Co-operative   *Continental*
8 Alvanley Terrace   *Corniche*
Whitehouse Loan   *Contour*
Edinburgh   *Cuillin*
1977-present day   *City*
                       Connection
                       Triathlon

J Edwards & Co   *Western*
Western Cycle Works
3-7 Gibson Street
Hillhead
Glasgow

George Elrick   *Elrick*
Lower Bridge Street
Stirling

Fairbairns
Edinburgh

Fairfield Cycle Co
Glasgow
1890s

91

Thomas Ferguson *Ferguson*
9a West Maitland Street
Edinburgh
Early twentieth century

William Flint *Forth*
2-3 Leith Street Terrace
Edinburgh
c1898

John Gair *Shetland Star*
85 King Harald Street
Lerwick
Shetland

Charles Gibb *Charles Gibb*
32 Victoria Street
Dundee
1930s-1950s

Glasgow Cycle Co *Argyle*
(later Argyle Cycles Ltd) *Waverley*
98 Commerce Street *Campbell of*
 Argyle
22 Farnell Street *White Heather*
Glasgow
1906-1970

Gordonson *Gordonson*
Wellington Street
Perth

John Victor Heininen
Kilrenny
Fife
c1906

Henderson Brothers *Sterling*
Ruthven Street
Auchterarder
Perthshire
Barnton Street
Stirling

Joe Hill
Glasgow

Howe Machine Co *Wizard*
Avenue Street *Record*
Bridgeton *Flying Scotchman*
Glasgow *Spider*
1872-1903 *Witch*
 Talisman
 Hercules
 Albemarle
 Alert
 Pioneer
 Scotch Express
 Avenue

P Jackson
31-33 Victoria Road
Dundee
c1905

Kilpatrick *Kilp*
Glasgow

King Fergie
Coatbridge

Kinnon Co *Levenvale*
Alexandria

D W Lindsay *Lindsay*
122 Victoria Road
Dundee
1930s-1960s

A B Louden *Persevere*
Jane Street
Leith
c1920

Alexander Luke
Newton Street
Duns
c1898

Neil McCulloch *McCulloch*
993 Govan Road
Glasgow

Andy McNeil *Andy McNeil*
Langlands Road
Glasgow
1950s

John & Andy McNeil   *McNeil Brothers*
925 Govan Road
Glasgow
1930s-1940s

John Melvin   *Melvin Champion*
Melvin Cycle Co
Alloa
Clackmannanshire
c1905

D Mudie   *Strathmore*
Eassie
Forfarshire
c1900

Myles
Hilltown
Dundee
1940s-1950s

Jack Nicholson   *Nicholson*
Forfar Road
15 Arbroath Road
Dundee

North Berwick Cycle Co   *Tantallon*
Foresters Hall Buildings
High Street
North Berwick
c1898

North British Machine Co Ltd
Carlton
19 Carlton Place
Glasgow
1930s

George Owen   *Standard*
69-81 Port Street
Stirling
c1904

Thomas Piper   *Merchiston*
41 Morningside Road
Edinburgh
1920s-1930s

John C Porter   *New Gerrard*
Greenside Place
Edinburgh

David Rattray & Co   *The Scot*
McCausland Street   *The Flying Scot*
253 Albert Street   *Queen of Scots*
7-11 Murray Street   *le' Ecosse*
86-88 Dalhousie Street   *Ventoux*
261 Alexandra Parade   *The Star*
254 High Street
Glasgow
1901-1981

T E & R S Richardson   *Edinburgh*
53 New Buildings   *Midlothian*
North Bridge   *Special Edinburgh*
Edinburgh   *Edinburgh Tricycle*
1870s/80s

Robertson Brothers   *Victor*
South Esplanade
Torry
Aberdeen
c1930

John Robertson   *Milano*
647 Govan Road   *Robertson*
Glasgow
1951-1960s

Robertson
Glasgow
c1900

Royal Cameron
Glasgow

George E Rutherford   *Dunedin*
2 Howard Place
23 Canonmills House
Edinburgh
1902-1922

St Vincent Cycles
242-245 St Vincent Street
Glasgow
c1907

Arthur Sangster   *The Speed*
379 George Street
Aberdeen
1899-1902

Thomas Shaw Ltd   *Oriel*
32 Reform Street
26 Ward Street
Dundee
c1908

Alexander Shiels   *Northern X*
258 West Crosscausway   *North Express*
Edinburgh

Malcolm C Smith   *Nightingale*
254 High Street
Glasgow
1920s-1950s

Sneddon   *Oriole*
Dundee
1990s

William Sorley   *Restalrig*
94 Duke Street
Manderston Street
Leith
c1914

Norrie Stark   *Club*
79 Rose Street   *RR*
116b Rose Street   *HM Tandem*
141 Dalry Road   *Club Tandem*
Edinburgh

John Stewart   *Spring-frame*
50 Polwarth Crescent
Edinburgh
c1902

George Sutherland   *Oases*
54 Raeburn Place
Edinburgh
c1905

James Sutherland   *Royal Fettes*
24 Home Street
54 Raeburn Place
Edinburgh

W R Tullock   *St Magnus*
Kirkwall Cycle and Motor Depot
Junction Road
Kirkwall
Orkney
c1910

Victoria Manufacturing Co   *Victoria*
78-82 Hanover Street
71 Cathedral Street
Glasgow
1890s-1920s

A S Valentine
Arbroath

Dave Walsh   *Dave Walsh*
Clarkston Cycle Centre
681 Clarkston Road
Netherlee
Glasgow
Present day

Wilson   *The Rosemount*
Alexandra Parade
Glasgow

Joseph Wood   *Norseman*
Kirkwall
Orkney

E & S Worrall   *Ridgity*
46-48 Duke Street
Hamilton
1930s-1960s

Makers of velocipedes

G Alsing
71 Sauchiehall Street
Glasgow

Anderson Brothers
93 Stockwell Street
Glasgow

Banks Brothers
King Street
Stirling

Thomas & John Bisset
J Bisset & Sons
Blairgowrie

Matthew Brown   *Edinburgh Tricycle*
57 St Leonard's Street
Edinburgh

James Gray
Milton of Campsie
Stirlingshire

David Low
Engineers
Losset
Alyth

Thomas McCall
Langlands Street
Kilmarnock

Marshall Brothers
73 Maxwell Street
Glasgow

Alexander Munro
Broughton Market
Edinburgh

Robert Pow
Selkirk

Adam Purves
Damside
Galashiels

T & F Smith   *Excelsior*
20 Great Clyde Street
Glasgow

Tommy Thompson
Stobs
Roxburghshire

James Watt
Biggar

Places to visit

Scottish museums with major cycle collections:

Alford, Aberdeenshire: Grampian Transport Museum
Elgin, Morayshire: Moray Motor Museum
Glasgow: Museum of Transport
Aberlady, East Lothian: Myreton Motor Museum
Edinburgh: National Museums of Scotland
Drumlanrig, Dumfries and Galloway: Scottish Cycle Museum
Many other Scottish museums include the occasional cycle in their general collections.

Further reading

The following selection of books covers general cycle and cycling history:

CLAYTON, N *Early Bicycles* (Shire Album 173) Aylesbury 1986
DODGE, P *The Bicycle* Paris & New York 1996
JONES, I K *The Safety Bicycle* (Shire Album 174) Aylesbury 1986
McGURN, J *On Your Bicycle* London 1987
RITCHIE, A *King of the Road* London 1975
STREET, R *The Pedestrian Hobby-Horse* Christchurch 1998

Clubs

There are many clubs throughout the UK covering almost every aspect of cycling interest. For those who are interested in cycling history and old bicycles it is recommended that they should join the Veteran-Cycle Club. The club has an active Scottish section that organises runs and events.

Contact: The Membership Officer,
Veteran-Cycle Club,
31 Yorke Road,
Croxley Green,
Rickmansworth,
Herts., WD3 3DW